BEER
Slabs, Stubbies and Six-Packs

BEER

Slabs, Stubbies and Six-Packs

Ben Canaider and Greg Duncan Powell

RANDOM HOUSE AUSTRALIA

Random House Australia Pty Ltd
20 Alfred Street, Milsons Point, NSW 2061
http://www.randomhouse.com.au

Sydney New York Toronto
London Auckland Johannesburg

First published by Random House Australia 2003

Copyright © Ben Canaider and Greg Duncan Powell, 2003

The Authors assert their moral rights to be identified as the Authors of this work.

All rights reserved. No part of this publication may be reproduced, stored in a retrieval system, or transmitted in any form or by any means, electronic, mechanical, photocopying, recording or otherwise, without the prior written permission of the publisher.

National Library of Australia
Cataloguing-in-Publication Entry

  Canaider, Ben
  Beer: slabs, stubbies and six-packs

  Includes index.
  ISBN 1 74051 255 3

  1. Beer - Australia. I. Powell, Greg Duncan. II. Title.

641.230994

Cover photography by Adrian Cook
Cover design by Darian Causby/Highway 51
Internal design and typesetting by Darian Causby/Highway 51
Printed and bound by Tien Wah Press (PTE) Limited, Singapore

10 9 8 7 6 5 4 3 2 1

To beer

Thanks for helping us through adolescence, for teaching us how to meditate, for giving us an understanding of women, and providing us with what self-confidence we have. Thanks for the blinders, the benders, the big nights out at the busiest end of the bar, the bands, the beer goggles and the big white telephone calls home . . .

Contents

Introduction 1
Beer Styles 4
Beer Ingredients 8
How Beer is Made 15
Glass Sizes 18
Chapter One · SESSIONAL BEERS 21
Chapter Two · PREMIUM BEERS 59
Chapter Three · BOUTIQUE BEERS 87
Chapter Four · HEAVY BEERS 99
Chapter Five · LIGHT BEERS 117
Chapter Six · WEIRDO BEERS 133
Glossary 159
Index 165

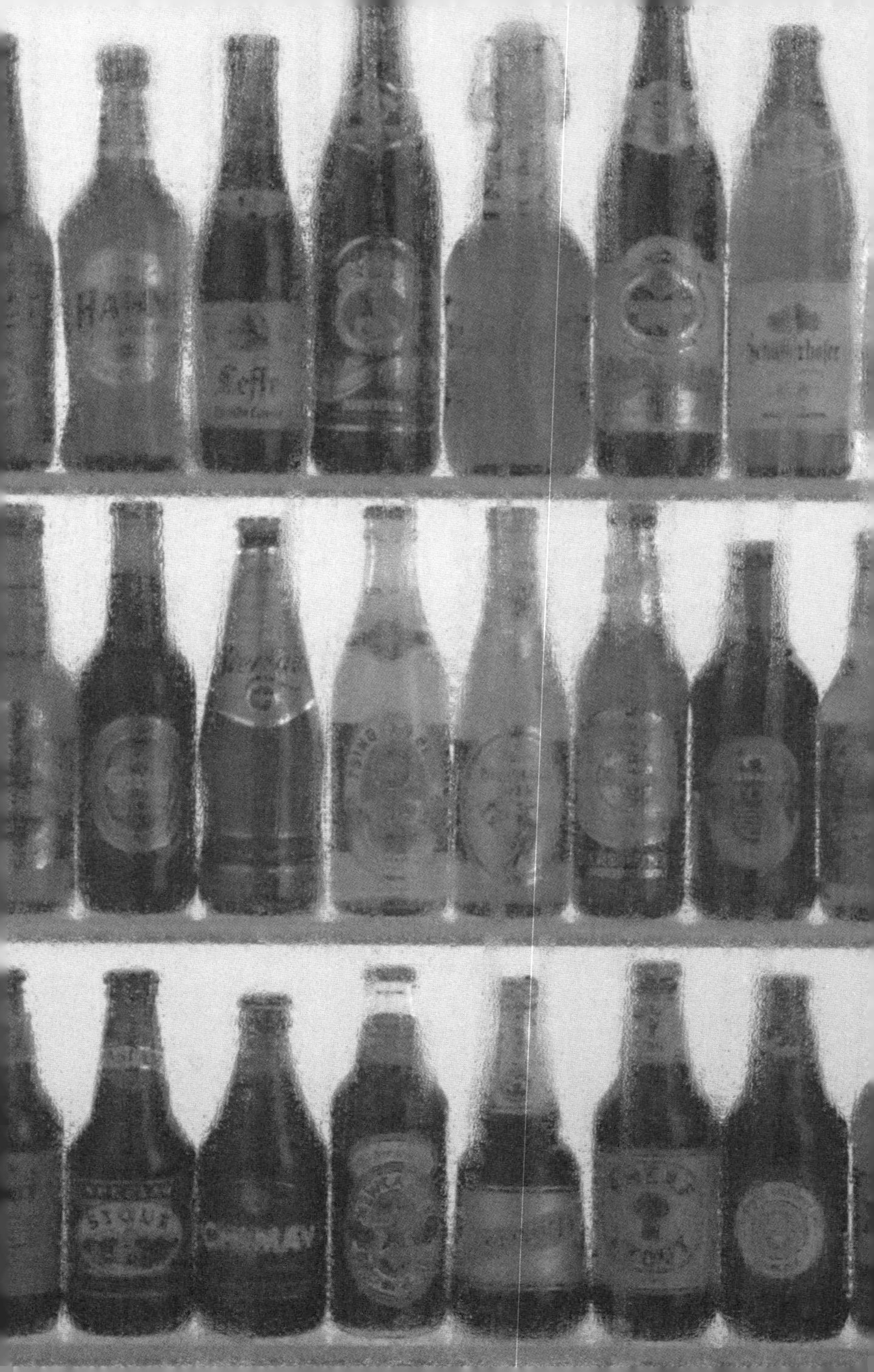
Leffe
STOUT
CHIMAY

Introduction

There is nothing more important to Australians than beer. Beer defines our state borders and lubricates the hinges of social (and sometimes sexual) relationships. It's everything. Even sport would be meaningless without beer — the drinking and the sponsorship. Beer defines us — both as a nation and individually. As Australians, we are very much what we drink.

Yet in a nation with a strong tradition of beer drinking, there is little or no information about beer — how it is produced, the ingredients that go into it, the style in which it's made, or how it should taste. These problems probably exist because beer drinkers don't go in for the kind of trainspotting that wine tossers do. Yet, in a strange way, this sort of navel gazing allows and encourages quality evaluation; it can help separate the good from the bad — a dog from a diamond.

It's necessary too, because things are changing. There are a lot more good beers around; the turf is becoming much more confusing. The terminology — such words as bitter, pilsener, lager, and ale — has been corrupted by marketing and sloganing and is no longer understood or correctly applied (if, indeed, it ever was). So maybe it's time for some standards, time for some clarity to help us understand and enjoy beer a little better. Most Australians don't even know the difference between ale and lager — the Adam and Eve of the beer world . . .

Is it perhaps because beer is for drinking and wine is for pontificating about? Well, we think it's a bit more complicated than that.

The boundary between the worlds of wine and beer is blurring. Wine is being quaffed; it's no longer just for doctors' and lawyers' dinner tables. Similarly, beer is being sipped — even appreciated; it's no longer just a drink for the masses. Thank goodness that just as we've entered the 21st century, Australians have finally begun to tear down those last remaining vestiges of a 19th-century English class system. It's OK to unthinkingly drink wine and there's nothing wrong with bringing some connoisseurship to beer.

Indeed, the beer drinker's timetable has changed. Beer is now consumed differently, and this guide seeks to map the changes and also, hopefully, point out the directions ahead. There are beers for sessional drinking — for heavy sessions — and we've got a chapter full of them in here. There are premium beers for those times when you just want one or two. There are beers for more thoughtful contemplation — the boutique ones. There are heavy beers, like stouts, which suit certain climes and times; and light beers for drivers that like to flavour their social life with beer. And there's also an ever-growing range of weirdo beers — both local and imported — that keep life interesting and keep the drinker asking the question, what is beer?

We wrote this book with a fridge full of beer, a laptop and a few CDs — Bruce Springsteen, Paul Weller, Tony Joe White, Elvis, and other great beer-drinking compilations. We tried to taste every beer made in or imported into Australia — from Foster's to the weirdest German doppel-bocks, Indian lagers to tasteless American crap . . . You won't find scores, stars or any other rating system, but if you read the review, we think you'll get the idea.

Chug-a-lug. Here's to beer.

Ben and Greg

Beer Styles

The beer children of this world are born of two parents: ales and lagers — the amber fluid's own Adam and Eve. Adam is the ale. He started it all and from him came lager — the missing rib, so to speak.

In Adam's world, the world of ales, Mother Nature naturally top-ferments malted barley. In ales we find the sustaining, chewy, fruity and almost old-world tasting beers. They are mostly described by colour, which is based on the type of malt they use. This also helps you to work out what sort of taste they'll provide. So we have pale ale, bottle-conditioned ale, amber ale, brown ale, dark ale, porters, and stouts — and (at the cloudy, pale end) wheat beers (they're top-fermenting too). Porters are a bit lighter than stouts, which have higher sugars, alcohol and hop bitterness to balance them out.

In lager land it's all a bit more complicated. It's like comparing the horse and carts of ales to lager's combustion engine. Refrigeration is critical to lager production (before refrigeration very cold caves had to suffice). The secret to lagers is not only lighter malts, but yeasts that work at lower temperatures over longer periods of time and at the bottom of the mixture. Lager's emphasis is thus on refreshment. From lagers come pilseners, bocks, draughts, bitters, lights, mid-strengths, dry lagers and cold-filtered products ...

Pilseners are perhaps the most widely misunderstood. They began in the town of Pilsen in Bohemia and were distinguished from lagers of the time by their extra hop bitterness and their pale golden colour. The local hops — Saaz — was critical to the style. True Pilseners are serious beers; to be made and to be taken so.

As you can see, lagers are complicated, mainly because many styles are misnamed, or take their names from old-fashioned beer-verbiage, like 'draught'. Bitters haven't always been bitter (see VB), and pilseners aren't always true to that style (see Reschs Pilsener...)

No wonder no one really knows what they are drinking. To help you sort out all this nonsense, here's a glossary of beer styles (as used or referred to in this book) and some examples found in Australia.

Ale: broad term for all beer and more specifically one half of the entire beer family. Ales are chewy and are made by a faster fermentation process. They satisfy more than they refresh, as opposed to lagers. Examples include: Coopers Sparkling, Coopers Pale Ale, Boddingtons, Chimay, Guinness — yes, they're all ales, generally speaking.

Amber Ale: ale with the colour slightly ramped up — thanks to the addition of a few more dark or golden malts. James Squire Original Amber Ale is a good example.

Bitter: a type of lager with more hop bitterness; for instance, Melbourne Bitter.

Bock: a more alcoholic and sweet malty lager from Germany. Beware. Paulaner Salvator.

Bottle-conditioned Ale: an ale that's undergone secondary fermentation in the bottle, to give it its carbonation. Coopers Sparkling and Pale Ales are examples.

Brown Ale: another step up from amber ale. Often with more alcohol. See Leffe Radieuse.

Cold-filtered: chilling heavily or freezing a beer after fermentation and before bottling to stabilise, clarify, smooth out, and often — we think — fuck a beer . . . Carlton Cold.

Dark Ale: nearly porter. James Squire's Porter is an example.

Draught: beers hand-pumped from casks; a type of horse nowadays used for promotional purposes; a generic name for a lot of lager.

Dry lager: a beer in which all the fermentable sugars have been eaten by the yeasts; a beer termed 'dry' but which is often not really so — residual sweetness is masked by hop fakery.

India Pale Ale: pale ale style with extra hops.

Lager: one half of the beer world; crisp, bottom-fermented beer. VB, Tooheys New, Fosters, Hahn Ice, Carlton Draught, Reschs Pilsener, XXXX Bitter, Melbourne Bitter.

Light: alcohol-reduced beer. Foster's Light Ice.

Mid-strength: a lager beer of about 3 to 4% alcohol by volume.

Pale Ale: top-fermented beer; pale in colour as opposed to the darker brown of normal ales. Cooper's Pale Ale.

Pilsener: a type of lager with a stronger hop accent. James Squire Pilsener, Pilsner Urquell (the original), Hahn Premium, Cascade Premium.

Porter: a dark ale on the way to becoming a stout.

Stout: a top-fermented, black-brown ale made from highly roasted malts.

Wheat Beer: beer made from not just barley but wheat as well. Yes, wheat beers. Here barley is replaced by wheat, making for a whole different range of flavours. In the northern hemisphere these are brewed as summer drinking beers; the tradition is starting to take off here, as with Hahn Witbier.

OK, enough. If we can get you to differentiate between ales and lagers then we reckon we've done a good job.

Beer Ingredients

Put simply, beer is made from the four ingredients of malt, hops, yeast and water. Other ingredients do exist however – the adjuncts and the enhancers.

ADJUNCTS

Generally speaking, an adjunct is something used as a substitute for malt; in most cases though it's usually used in conjunction with malt. The role of such adjuncts is threefold. They help bring the cost of brewing down (malt is expensive); they can be used to manipulate flavour; and sometimes they're used because there's simply not enough malted barley to go around.

The most common adjunct is sugar. It raises the alcoholic content of beer without adding any flavour. Corn is also a popular one, particularly in big corn-growing countries like America where it sometimes accounts for up to 50% of the mash. Then there's rice, not surprisingly a popular adjunct in Asian countries. Extracted malts are sometimes used, just like the stuff home-brewers employ.

ENHANCERS

Before hopping became common practice, many brewers relied on flavour enhancers to give their beer a bit of extra oomph – or, probably more likely, to cover some dud notes. Such things as honey and chilli have been used; and fruits like cherries, apples, bananas and orange and lemon peel, too; then there are herbs and spices like ginger. If you want to try a good example of a flavour-enhanced beer have a go at Hoegaarden White, which is a wheat beer flavoured with coriander seed and citrus peel.

MALT

Everything needs a building block. For beer it is malt – malted barely. You can make beer out of other starches – rice, wheat, corn, cornflakes, Uncle Toby's muesli, et cetera – but six millenniums of brewing has proved malted barley is best.

But where does malt come from? It starts in a paddock with barley. The best stuff goes to maltsters for beer making; the rest goes to cattle feed. (In the end, barley sustains both man and beast. Beer glass or cattle trough, it's the same thing.)

There are many types of barley – two row, six row, and varieties like Golden Promise and Mendip Gold – but beer drinkers are not the geeks that wine tossers are, and this sort of information tends not to interest. Barley becomes malt . . . OK, next please.

But hang on; malt is not just grains of barely. It's grains of barley giving birth – or germinating. The process is controlled by a maltster (in pictures these blokes normally have a shovel) who will partially dry the barley in order to eliminate the risk of mould or premature germination (that's *germination* . . .). Next, the barley is steeped in water, which gets the seed growing. Now it undergoes more drying in a kiln. This amount of cooking — or kilning — will determine how dark or coffee-ed the malt gets. When you make cute girlie lager you want pale malt; when you make stout you need malt that's been roasted to within an inch of its life.

There are quite a few types of malt, and brewers can use a mix of them to achieve more complex flavours. There can be six or seven different malts in a brew. Pale malt is slowly kilned over a day or two. Amber and brown malts are cooked at higher temperatures. Crystal malt is cooked in a very fast-acting kiln, which crystallises the sugary core. Chocolate malt is kilned more steadily and for a longer time to get the roasted, nutty flavours. And finally, black malt is the stuff that you accidentally leave on the stove...

But why do blokes and blokettes making beer frig around germinating barley? They're not going to plant it, are they? Actually, germination has another purpose: it helps release enzymes that convert the grain's starch into fermentable sugar. And as everyone knows, you can't have alcohol without sugar; therefore, you can't have beer without malt.

HOPS

Hops are to beer what salt is to food. Interestingly, however, while beer has been around for 6000 years, hops only came on the scene about 900 years ago. Monks had mucked around putting hops into their brews from the 8th century but it was a chick — a nun called Hildegard — who was the first to actually note the positive effect of hops added to beer. She was making 'medicinal' brews at the time and observed how hops stabilised the finished product, preventing it from going off. She said nothing about the taste however. Spices and herbs had been used for a similar effect, but as from Hildegard, hops took over.

The hop itself is the flower of a feisty perennial vine. It's related to cannabis, but it's a bit harder to grow. It prefers cooler latitudes and won't climb of its own accord. It has to be painstakingly trained up wires each year. During its growing season the vine can put on a metre of growth in three days. There are male and female varieties, but it's the girl flowers — or cones, as they are known (another cannabis reference) — that the brewer is interested in. To be more precise, it's the cone's yellowy resin (known as lupulin) that is the active ingredient. This is an oil exclusive to hops and containing high alpha acids. Alpha acids are bitter, so hopped beer is bitter.

There are many types of hops, and brewers play with these to impart different aromas, flavours and levels of bitterness. In Bavaria, Germany's most famous hop-growing region, Hallertau dominates. Czech pilseners owe their distinctive aromas to Saaz. Pride of Ringwood is an Australian hop developed by the CSIRO — it is high in alpha acids ...

In Australia hops are grown in the cooler bits of Victoria and Tasmania. And if you're ever in Hobart in March, head out to Bushy Park and check out the hop harvest. Most hop cones are not used fresh, however. The cones are dried, powdered, and turned into pellets that look a bit like chook feed. Or the hop oil can be extracted. These processes enable breweries all over the world to use a plethora of hop varieties, if they so wish.

It is a truly amazing plant — a preservative, a flavouring agent and even a sedative. Years ago there were such things as hop pillows. If you couldn't sleep, a pillowcase was stuffed full of fresh hop flowers and that would send you to nigh-nighs. Nowadays, a cure for insomnia is to ingest hops orally, with alcohol, in the form of beer . . .

YEAST

Yeast is like petrol. Put petrol in your car and it provides burning rubber, tyre smoke and the screech of wheels. Put yeast into a brewing kettle and it produces alcohol and carbon dioxide. Both yeast and petrol fuel young men's often-dangerous escapist fantasies: sinking stubbies or dropping doughnuts. It gets more dangerous still when the two combine — so never put yeast in your petrol tank.

Just as there are many different types of petrol — unleaded, lead-replacement, high-octane, super-premium, expensive, cheap or watered-down — there are many different types of yeast. And they probably provide brewers with their most difficult professional challenges. Like any living creature, yeast does not have one day exactly like the next — nor is it always on its best behaviour. It's fickle: it responds to different environments, yet in the same environment will act differently — converting sugars to alcohol at different speeds, not doing anything at all, dying prematurely, or making bad smells (those slightly dodgy esters that many beers contain). In an effort to seek some kind of control in the never-ending experiment that is beer making, over the last 130 years brewers and scientists — like the famous Louis Pasteur — have isolated particular yeast strains that have a more helpful disposition. Another great bloke was Emil Hansen, who, at the Carlsberg brewery in Copenhagen in the late 1870s, was able to break down yeasts into single strains. This achievement meant brew dependability became more of a reality. More recently still, brewers have played with yeasts that ferment beer without producing so much alcohol, and this has helped to improve the taste and body of light-alcohol beer.

The main yeast in beer making, known as brewers yeast (or *Saccharomyces Cerevisiae*), loves nothing better than to replicate itself in a sugar-rich environment. In fact, it would be quite nice to come back in the next life as *Saccharomyces C.* You get to root your brains out for over a week in a brewery where every gorgeous little malt sugar is as attractive as the last — or the next. Then you die a beautiful death — rising to the top of the brew as if to heaven, or falling gently to the bottom for peace eternal. What's more, life has not been meaningless — you've created beer...

And one other thing, in bottle-fermented ales — like Coopers Sparkling and Pale — the dead yeast that has fallen to the bottom of the beer is one of Mother Nature's elixirs. Full of vitamin B, it is alleged to prevent the effects of hangovers. Rest in Yeast.

WATER

Many beer drinkers are shocked to learn that the beer they buy is up to 97% water. But water is critical to every aspect of beer, even drinking it — not to mention washing up the glasses.

Before reticulated town-water supplies, breweries were usually sited near a clear and pure water source. The very first pilsener achieved its fame partly because the water that went into it was so good. Even today in Australia the purity of Cascade's Tasmanian water lends a certain cachet to the beer. On the other hand, CUBs don't tend to advertise the fact that their main beer mega-factory is situated on Melbourne's Yarra River...

Of course, the reality is that all modern brewers tend to adjust water before it meets the malt. Bicarbonate, sodium, chloride, calcium, magnesium, zinc, sulphate... All these components are analysed and, if necessary, fiddled with. If town water is being used, the chlorine and fluoride are taken out. The type of water can also be adjusted to the style of beer: soft water is best for lagers; water with a high mineral component is good for ales.

Indeed, in a brewery, water is not just water; brewers even give it their own name: they call it not H_2O, but liquor. Perhaps they call it liquor because they only ever tend to take water with whisky? As we know, drinking water only makes you rust — look what it does to radiators . . .

How Beer is Made

As any honest, modest home-brewer will tell you, making beer is really not that hard. Here's the basic recipe:

Step One

Prepare your water. Filter it to remove chlorine and fluoride and all the other things water companies put in it. Then adjust the minerals and salts to suit your brew (as discussed in the Beer Ingredients chapter). Don't, however, believe any crap about water being everything to a brew. It might be 95% of the beer that you drink, but if it was so good you wouldn't be turning it into beer, would you?

Step Two

Get your malted barley of the type you prefer (remember, dark malts for stouts, pale malts for lagers). Crush it up. Malt comes from a maltster. These fellows tend to have apocryphal names like Joe White — the bloke who supplies the malt for most of Australia's beers. Crushing smashes the husk and helps release the starch for Step Three . . .

Step Three
The crushed malt goes into a big kettle of hot water and is mixed around — as you would with porridge — until you've made a mash.

Step Four
The next step is to separate the grain husks from the pure malt and water mixture — the 'wort'. This is one of the reasons why barley is such a fantastic grain to use. Its husks act as a filter for all the unwanted rubbish as the wort drains through. This is known as lautering, from the German word meaning to filter; it takes place in a Lautertun. Yes, brewing is full of old Anglo-Saxon and German words.

Step Five
The malt and water infusion, or wort, is now boiled together with the hops — a seasoning that's one of beer's most important ingredients. This process ensures that the sweet richness of the malt is counter-balanced by the sharp bitterness of the hops. Just as in cooking, timing is crucial: too little and you won't extract all the flavour and bitterness you require; too much and your hops — like overcooked vegetables — lose their delicacy and flavour.

Step Six
You now have something to ferment. Bring the hops/malt infusion down to a yeast-tolerant temperature (anywhere from 12 to 30 degrees Centigrade, depending on whether you're making lagers or ales) and chuck in the said yeast. Fermentation time, temperature, and the type of yeast used all have an important effect on the resultant beer's smells and flavours.

Step Seven
The final trick can either make or break a beer and yet it involves the brewer doing nothing at all — except being patient. The fermented beer is left to sit around and mature. This process is called conditioning. It helps clarify the beer and give it bubbles, or its head.

Step Eight
After conditioning you have what brewers call 'a bright beer'; that is, a beer ready for final filtering, pasteurisation, bottling, kegging, labelling, selling, profit-making, et cetera.

Step Nine
Drinking. Open bottle, pour into mouth (remembering to open mouth), swallow . . .

Glass Sizes

As often as you hear blokes standing around in pubs talking about who won the premierships in the 1980s or how many times Steve Waugh got out in the 1990s, you'll invariably hear them rattling on about different names for different beer-glass sizes in the different states of Australia. Glass sizes began in fluid ounces — the old imperial measure — so there are some minor discrepancies in modern metric equivalents. Here's the breakdown:

New South Wales
Pony: 140ml
Glass: 200ml
Middy: 280ml
Schooner: 420ml

Queensland
Small beer: 140ml
Beer: 240ml
Pot: 280ml

South Australia
Butcher: 170ml
Schooner: 250ml
Pint: 420ml

Tasmania
Four: 120ml
Six: 170ml
Eight: 240ml
Ten: 280ml

(The names of these glass sizes reflect the old imperial ounce measurements.)

Victoria
Pony: 120ml
Glass: 200ml
Pot: 280ml

Western Australia
Pony: 120ml
Glass: 140ml
Middy: 200ml
Pot: 280ml

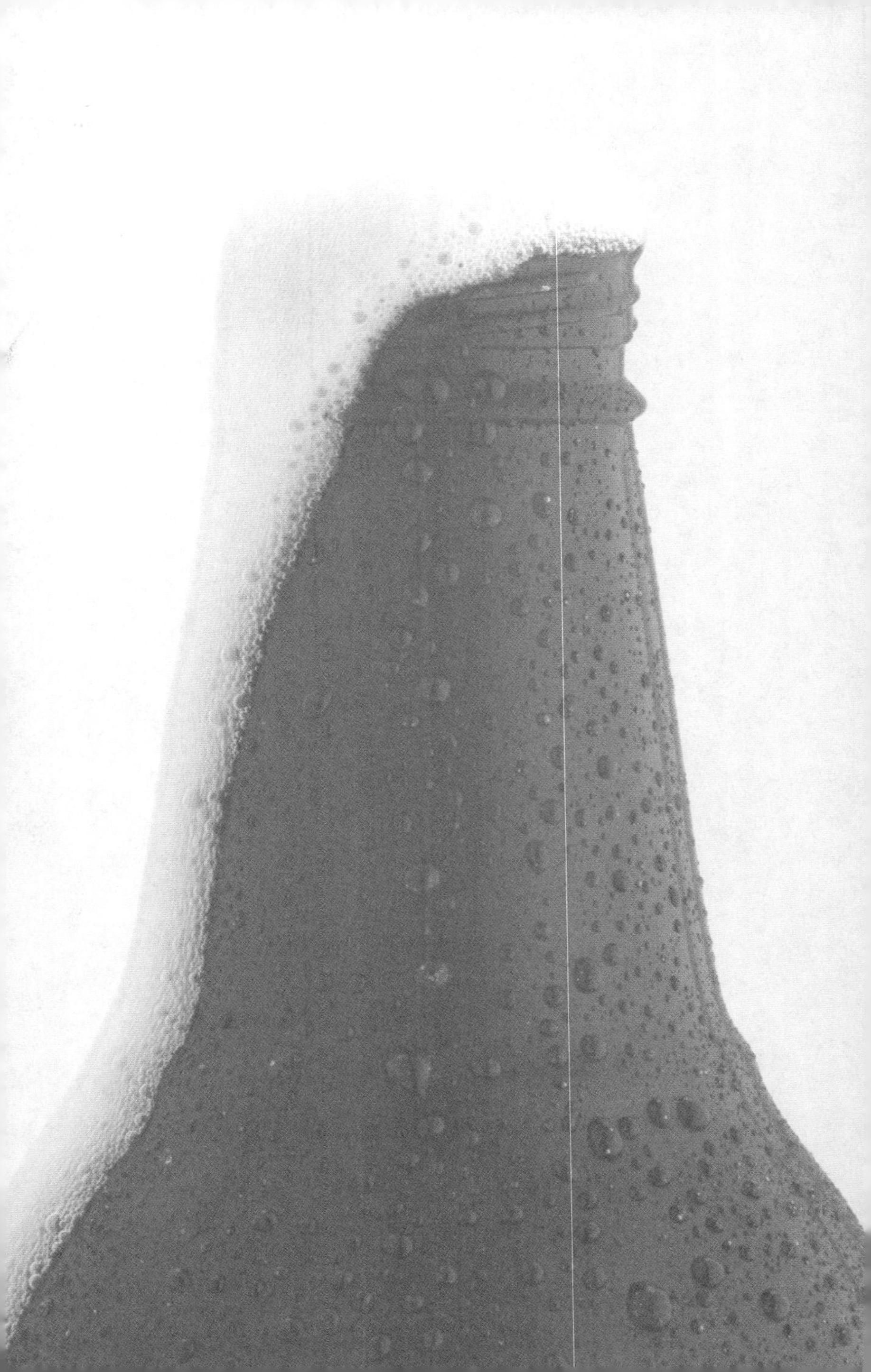

Chapter One
Sessional Beers

Australians love a good session, whether it's in the pub, in front of the telly, or in the bedroom. When it comes to television, cricket's the pinnacle. Essentially nothing happens: 22 men dirty their whites over a five-day period. Perfect television. In the bedroom, well, it doesn't last as long as a Test match, but we don't really believe that Aussie men are bad lovers . . . And in the pub, we drink sessional beers.

But what is a sessional beer? It's something you can drink over and over again without it ever losing its pleasure. Like watching Dennis Lillee walk back to his mark time and time again; like exploring the unexpurgated version of your significant other's sexual fantasies; or sinking beer after beer after beer after beer down the pub with Wayne, Tripod and Trev.

Sessional beers run a fine line. They can't be so demanding that they give you beer fatigue after only two glasses, but they need to taste like something. Otherwise, what's the point? You might as well drink mineral water. Sessional beers are beers you enjoy drinking — thoughtlessly. Twenty of them . . .

To make a sessional beer is harder than you think. Malt and hops and water when fermented together produce strong flavours. After all, beer is often considered to be a food. Luckily, Australian brewers have long been geared towards the production of extremely drinkable beers. They've had to be, because Australian drinkers have demanded such drinks. Unlike Belgian Trappist monks who would reverently work their way through one life-sustaining, faith-inducing beer of the Lord, Australian drinkers have traditionally applied themselves to beer with the sort of abandon you'd expect in a country that invented the slab and the long weekend. (Slab: unit of measure; amount of beer required by one man for one night/barbecue/family function/bushfire.)

In this sense, sessional beers are the true social lubricants of our society. The best ones are like background music. They fill in the blank spaces, make for a convivial atmosphere, but don't get in the way of conversation. Good session brews are beers with the volume turned down. They hint at richness without being sweet, they're dry without being too bitter, and they finish like an episode of a really good mini-series — with you hanging out to see the next show.

Of course you can interpret sessional beers as being cynical — in fact, even a little bit evil. They're made deliberately so that you drink another one and another one and another one. Sessional beers can lead to the disease known as sessional drinking, and sessional drinkers can reach the state where they don't care what they're pouring down their throats. We're not telling you to give up a good session, but don't lose your sense of appreciation. That could lead to you hating sex, or worse still . . . cricket.

Asahi Super "Dry"

Lager 330ml 5% alc vol

This is Ben's favourite sessional beer. When he hasn't had beer for a while, when he's been drinking wine or other beer all day, or when he's been on a gin binge, Asahi is the product he turns to. He can always manage to fit one more in. But why is it so good? Well, it has flavour — that real 'premium', even Germanic, malty aroma, without the weight and flavour in the mouth that normally brings. There's a hoppy zing, good balance, but, best of all, it slides down the throat so effortlessly. The only way you can tell Asahi is Japanese is from the faintest whiff of rice cake . . .

And another thing . . .

Asahi is more Japanese than it tastes. It has all the hallmarks of fine German pilsener, but Japanese technology and innovation have taken it one step further. It's like comparing a top-of-the-range Honda to a BMW. And just as the Mazdas we drive are now made in Thailand, so too is the Asahi we drink here.

Beck's Beer

Pilsener 330ml 5% alc vol

Beck's is arguably Germany's best-known exported beer. It's a straightforward, dryish, popular Pilsener. It owes its popularity to its rather unusual thumbprint. Beck's is bipolar. On the one hand it has a little bit of that typical German rich malt and exotica, on the other hand it slips across the palate like a simple dry beer. If you're into analysing beers, Beck's might taste a bit awkward, but if you're just into sucking them up you won't notice.

And another thing . . .

Beck's is Germany's most exported beer. It is to German beer what Kylie Minogue is to Australian music. Both are not consumed as much in their homelands as they are internationally. Neither truly represents their native countries any more. Kylie doesn't play pub rock and Beck's isn't drunk in German pubs.

Boag's Strongarm Bitter

Lager 375ml 5.2% alc vol

With a label that looks like it's been drawn by the work experience kid (it's actually an old advertisement), Strongarm disappoints before you even get the cap off. It's a rather weak link in the otherwise impressive chain of James Boag's beers. What struck us about it was its clumsiness. A yeasty and weirdly tropical fruity smell introduces a fairly dumb and bitsy one-dimensional beer flavour. An awkward lump of malt sits right in the middle of your tongue and the beer finishes in a sour, watery, bar-towel sort of way. Stick to Boag's Original.

And another thing . . .

Sometimes we reckon brewers think that there's a section of the beer-drinking market that doesn't know or doesn't deserve any better than this. 'Don't challenge them, don't rock the boat!' seems to be the creed. We know brewers can do better. Times are changing, Mr Boag.

Boddingtons Pub Ale

Ale 440ml 4.7% alc vol

This fully imported can of classic, velvety English ale is all freshness, well-mimicked cask conditioning, and quenching bitterness. The head has the white and fluffy texture of a kid's cartoon cloud. The colour is a bright amber, and the overall effect is thoroughly enticing. It's a class act. There's waxy honey, stewed apples, a little bit of toffee and a beautiful soft-dry finish. The considerable bitterness only registers quite some time after you've swallowed. There's not too much fizz so you can slam it down fast. For ale addicts, this is a veritable Red Cross parcel.

And another thing . . .

Many people are disappointed by their first taste of imported English beer, finding it a bit soapy, a bit flat and just a bit dull. It seems to lack the crisp refreshment of heavily chilled Australian lagers. Part of the problem is that it rarely simulates the real thing — hand-pumped, cask-conditioned real ale. Boddos does it better than most.

Caffrey's Premium Beer

Brown Ale 440ml 4.2% alc vol

A widget-assisted ale, Caffrey's pours from the tin to reveal a golden-brown colour topped and contrasted with an attractive white creamy head. But that's as good as it gets. It is indeed a pretty understated beer. Simple smells of dried banana chip precede a fairly thin and watery mouthful of simple, slightly bitter ale. It probably tastes fantastic in a pub in Ireland but here in our Melbourne office it's a bit disappointing. Best served very chilled on a hot, steamy day when you need nothing more than a thirst quencher.

And another thing . . .

Irish ales are very much second fiddle (if you'll pardon the pun) to classic dry Irish stouts. The best ales still come from England, but as English sporting teams know only too well, you can't be good at everything. The Irish have got stouts covered, and that's enough.

Carlton Cold

Lager 375ml 4.7% alc vol

With CUB's characteristic sweet-and-sour nose, Carlton Cold manages to magnificently replicate the look, flavour, texture and finish of mediocre Victorian pub tap beer. Quite an achievement — and possibly a reason for its popularity. What you don't get with this beer, however, is the conviviality of the main bar, Sky Tab, the ever-increasing beauty of the barmaid, or the unmentionables of the men's dunny. Without all that what's the point of this beer?

And another thing . . .

We think we know how this packaging came about. The marketing geniuses decided that we wanted a stubby in a clear bottle that screamed out 'Freshness!' It reminds us more of the stubbies in the bottom of the ice-filled bath: their labels washed off, ending up somehow wrapped around the top of the bottle, making it just that little bit more frustrating when you try to remove the cap.

Carlton Draught

Lager 375ml 4.7% alc vol

The smell of this beer reminds us of a walk through the car wreckers on a wet day: rusting panels, hollowed-out wrecks, UV-damaged vinyl, empty petrol tanks, and a hint of sump oil. No wonder it's the beloved brew of hoons throughout Victoria. It's lightly bodied, very sessional, and has a lick of syrupy malt painted over with a bitter metallic hop finish. And if we could get the Carlton Draught colour in a spray can, no car would be safe.

And another thing . . .

Carlton Draught drinkers think they know more about beer than their mates. To them Foster's is a kid's drink, VB is for private school poofters, Melbourne Bitter is OK — when there's no Draught around — but Carlton is tougher, harder and gruffer. Of course, none of this thinking bears any relationship to actual flavour. Isn't beer fantastic?!

Cascade Pale Ale

Lager 375ml 5% alc vol

This pale-ale-style beer combines a sense of ale's chewy texture with the clean, cool freshness of a fine lager. It's a crossover beer. The smell reminds us of dewy morning paddocks and mossy rocks by fresh streams. The malt sits well to the background, a support not a feature. Like an ale it does go down the throat with a glug. You have to swallow it – it doesn't slip down. The hops have the requisite high notes as well as roasted-nut oiliness. This is the thinking person's sessional beer.

And another thing . . .

We've talked a lot about the two families of the beer world – ales and lagers. There's a third one you need to know about. It's a hybrid of the first two, a style that picks the best out of both. It's a lager made with an ale in mind. Refreshing but natural tasting. Brewing technology is always blurring the beer world's boundaries.

Coopers Original Pale Ale

Pale Ale 375ml 4.5% alc vol

This beer doesn't taste contrived. It's as if it makes itself. Completely free of additives and preservatives, this full, fruity, pale ale has an enticing sweet-and-sour nose followed by an explosive, refreshing, yet at the same time satisfying, sustaining flavour. It's one of those beers that once you've acquired a taste for it, you're addicted. As far as sessional beers go, Coopers Pale is king. Ben knows, he lived in Adelaide for a while and lived on the stuff.

And another thing . . .

When you go to a bar in Adelaide and order a Coopers stubby, the barman, before removing the cap, will invert the bottle and gently turn it around in his hand, thus mixing the yeast sediment in the bottle's base through the ale. But why? Because of the Vitamin B in the dead yeast cells left over from the bottle-conditioning carbonation process. Mother Nature's Berocca. And they say you don't get hangovers on Coopers Pale . . . bullshit.

Corona Extra

Lager 330ml 4.6% alc vol

Corona is more than just a trend among poofs and inner-city types who enjoy enthusiastically poking quartered limes into the top of the bottle, their biggest concern being whether to stick it all the way in or leave a little bit jutting out . . . No, Corona's more than this. It has a place and sessionability that recommends it strongly to long, hot Australian summers. Pale yellow in colour, with hops, malt, a bit of honey, and lemon-tree foliage for aroma, its body is a delicate silhouette, outlining the beer like a sombrero-wearing gringo on the horizon at sunset.

And another thing . . .

Corona's packaging absolutely nails it. The tall, thin, long-necked bottle; the stencilled, simple two-colour label; the olde-worlde Spanish font; the duelling iguanas; and the porthole in the middle. Even if you don't like this beer, it's a good beer to be seen with. Indeed, many people don't think of this as beer but more as a fashion accessory.

Emu Bitter

Lager 375ml 4.6% alc vol

A very impressive sessional beer is Emu Bitter. From its enticing yellowy-golden colour, which seems to promise freshness, to its characterful, earthy-cum-estuary smell, here's a bitter which is . . . bitter. The brewers didn't stint in the addition of hops; remember, it's hops that make bitterness — and balance. This beer tastes a bit rustic, as if it wasn't made in a factory by a huge multinational company. And it tastes like it wasn't made with perfect, multi-filtered, mineral-adjusted water, either. It's an emu by the billabong.

And another thing . . .

There's a lot of crap written these days about beer-and-food matching. Wine-and-food matching is bad enough, so why should poor old beer have to suffer the same disease? When you have a good bitter beer like this with fish and chips it's just a matter of refuelling and being refreshed. Some beer styles do suit some types of food better than others, but let's not get too anal . . .

Foster's Lager

Lager 355ml 4.9% alc vol

'Foster's Lager, it's got the flavour that's taking it all around the world.' But what is that flavour? It's a flavour that is supremely inoffensive; indeed, it is what Foster's *isn't* that recommends it. It has a generic golden-yellow lager colour, a faintly fruity lager aroma, heavily subdued or possibly sedated malt, and a hint of hop bitterness. It tiptoes across your palate as if it doesn't want to wake up your senses. Like we said, it's supremely inoffensive.

And another thing . . .

How bizarre are some of Australia's most successful exports? INXS, the Crocodile Hunter, Clive James, John Pilger, Germaine Greer, our own Kylie, and, of course, Foster's Lager. What do all these things have in common? It's too nightmarish to contemplate.

SESSIONAL BEERS / 35

Hahn Ice

Lager 345ml 4.2% alc vol

This is straightforward, almost characterless, cute lager. Made by the ice-brewing process (more of which below), there's nothing wrong with it, but it's a bit like one of those television presenters who looks the part, speaks clearly, yet doesn't have much personality. He certainly won't ever have his own show or run a telethon. He might end up doing a few car yard ads, or even endorse the odd slimming product, but that's it. And that's it for this beer, too. It's a kind of thoughtless way of getting beer into you.

And another thing . . .

And that's the point of the ice-brewing process. After the beer is fermented it's frozen, which cleans up the beer and smoothes it out. It's a bit like a beer lobotomy. You lose harsh flavours but you lose the personality as well. Ice beers are terribly popular and clear bottles very trendy. They say a clear bottle indicates how seriously the brewer treats the beer. . .

Holsten Premium Bier

Pilsener 330ml 5% alc vol

This light pilsener style is ideal for sessional drinkers. It will appeal to the sort of bloke who likes the extra anchovies on pizza and hates birthday cake. Let's call him Trevor. He thinks Victoria Bitter is misnamed — it might come from Victoria but it's not bitter. That's why he's drinking Holsten. It smells herbal and a little rusty, with a trace of simple, supermarket honey. It's smoothly flavoured but not big-bodied. Its main feature is its finish — more hop bitterness. After the sixth Holsten Trev's mouth feels as clean as a whistle — and ready for the seventh.

And another thing . . .

Holsten claims to be a true lager, which means that it's fermented slowly at nearly freezing temperatures for up to a month. We reckon it's more in the pilsener style though. Remember, pilseners are part of the lager family but they have just a bit more malty richness and hop bitterness. And like most German lagers, Holsten claims to be Germany's biggest seller.

J.Boag's Original Bitter

Lager 375ml 4.7% alc vol

This serious sessional bitter is worthy of its name – original. There's something honest and old world about its understated package and honest generosity. You get shitloads of flavour here, both in the malt and hop departments. The maltiness almost overflows; it's like Cornwell's Extract of Malt (if you can remember that stuff). This is balanced, however, by some firm, bittering hops at the steely rather than spicy end of the spectrum. Everyone who meets the 'Original' for the first time is invariably struck by the full-on flavours.

And another thing . . .

While writing this book, it struck us how some of the best beers in Australia (Emu Bitter, Boag's Original) are so unbelievably unpopular and hard to get. Sometimes we wonder if they are deliberately kept from a wider audience in order not to show up the shithouseness of our mainstream amber staples.

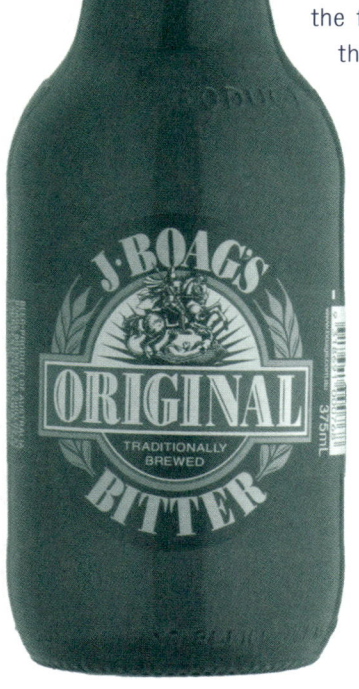

Kilkenny Draught

Ale 440ml 4.3% alc vol

In many ways Kilkenny strikes us as being the widget-powered, canned equivalent of the global Irish-theme-pub epidemic. The side of the can tells you that this beer has its origins in a 12th-century Franciscan abbey in Kilkenny. Crap. It was, in fact, invented in 1987 by a brewing company called Smithwicks. Not that there's anything wrong with that except that the beer's not too flash. It smells of Bonox, beef stock cubes and Vegemite. It's creamy and lactic, with a bitter and slightly hard finish. There are better widget-powered British beers.

And another thing . . .

We did a little postmortem on our can of Kilkenny and compared the widget inside to some other widget-powered products. There are aesthetic differences but they're slight. The principle is the same. A little plastic device about the size of a large gallstone gases the beer when you open it. Isn't technology wonderful?

Melbourne Bitter

Lager 375ml 4.9% alc vol

Melbourne Bitter is the non-identical twin brother to VB. While VB has had heaps of success with its sweet, smooth style, Melbourne is a little more cynical and bitter. It has a starker personality and therefore less popularity. The family trait — that CUB sweet-and-sour yeast-and-hop gene — is probably at its most obvious in Melbourne Bitter. Simple lumpy malt flavours are brought to a prickly, bitter finish, and MB's lingering afterthought is an unresolved struggle of the family legacy — sweet or sour?

And another thing . . .

One of the thought-provoking parts of Australian beer culture has been the use of primary colours in identifying different products. The CUB siblings VB and Melbourne Bitter could only be mistaken by the visually impaired, and Cascade's Red, Blue and Green were supposedly different beer styles but many Hobartians just drank their favourite colour. We wonder how pink packaging would go?

Miller Genuine Draft

Lager 355ml 4.7% alc vol

This is a harmless enough beer-like product — cold-filtered to within an inch of its life to remove all those beer flavours that have for so many thousands of years made people want to drink beer. With lemony hops, the faintest hint of malt, and the slightest nuance of raw peanuts just at the back of the mouth, everything in this beer is in the background — you really have to look for it. This is beer with the volume turned right down. Really, you might as well take it in tablet form.

And another thing . . .

While cold-filtering a beer after fermentation does tend to turn it into a more accessible product, it does mean that the beer doesn't have to be pasteurised (that is, cooked) before bottling. Both cold-filtering and pasteurisation are forms of stabilisation, and for mass-market, global products, stabilisation is a necessary evil.

Newcastle Brown Ale

Brown Ale 330ml 4.7% alc vol

The colour of mahogany-stained architraves, 'Newie' is a good introduction to English ales. It's attractive in the glass, smooth to drink, and not too bitter. There is the whiff of fully integrated steely hops when you first raise the glass from the bar, but there are other more interesting smells: a bit of dried banana, wet gravel, Anzac biscuits (don't ask us how they got in there) and a bit of burnt toffee. The caramel toffee flavours continue across your tongue where you also find a textural tang that stops the Newie from being flabby. In the right conditions — cold weather, a dark night, football-crowd violence — you can drink yards and yards of this stuff.

And another thing . . .

A lot of English brown ales can seem too sweet, malty and dark in colour -- even a bit soapy. Newcastle's Brown has to appeal to two tastes, however, as Scotland is just over the border. Geordies refer to it as 'the dog' — as in 'Ahm just gan doon the rood to tak the dog for a walk.'

Old Speckled Hen

Brown Ale 355ml 5.2% alc vol

There's quite a lot of Rhode Island Red in this speckled hen's colour. From the yeast used it has an aroma of banana fritters on the barbie. The flavour relies more on sharp, hard, bittering hops. If you're a real hop-head you might get into this beer — particularly its long, bitter aftertaste. The body is quite light and most of the flavour falls on the tip of the tongue. We reckon this beer will do its best with greasy food. It's a sessional beer — but only if you can afford it. It's a bit pricey.

And another thing . . .

Some of you might think that this beer was named after a chook, maybe a bantam. How silly of you. It is, of course, named after a car that tooled around the beer's home town — Abingdon. A sports car. An MG. Its owner — obviously unable to win the attention he so desperately craved — painted it black and gold.

Reschs Original Pilsener

Pilsener 375ml 4.4% alc vol

Reschs Pilsener, the silver-bullet beer, is the first beer Greg ever drank, as a three-year-old. Had he never tasted any other beer he might have been able to survive on this stuff. But the reality is that in terms of quality and structure Reschs beers are being left behind by the competition. This one is another invertebrate — no backbone, no structure and it doesn't know the difference between its arse and its elbow. At best, it is beer-like.

And another thing . . .

There used to be a rumour going around New South Wales that when purchasing a middy in a bar you should go for Tooheys over Reschs because the latter's lines and taps were gunky. This, according to the rumour, accounted for Reschs distinctive taste. Having done the tasting of all these beers out of stubbies, we think it's just the way the beer is made.

Reschs Real

Pilsener 375ml 4.2% alc vol

There's not a lot to recommend Reschs Real. It smells like beery carpet and rusting concreter's reo. Even the colour looks a bit suspicious. It's short, dumb, dumpy and structureless. You get one lumpy bang of milky malt in the middle of your mouth followed by more rustiness from the hops. And as it flows over the tongue there's the impression that some of the alcohol has been removed. Real? More like unreal.

And another thing . . .

Tosspot drinks editors, such as ourselves, love to talk about the 'structure' of the beverages we analyse. Structure is like the skeleton from which all the flavours hang. A beer without structure is like a dead jellyfish — and you know what happens if you step on one of them at the beach.

San Miguel Super Dry

Dry Lager 330ml 4.8% alc vol

This beer's effortless drinkability makes it an ideal sessional brew. It's very light in weight and light in flavour, which is what super-dry beers are all about. It's almost like not drinking beer. Six or seven of these could go down the chute and the only way you'd know is that you'd be spending more time at the latrines. On the nose there's a hint of orange-blossom honey (but just a hint); the head dissipates quickly, and the palate is dry without bitter edges. It's the beer you drink when you're not drinking beer; ideal in humid, hot weather, and as hair of the dog.

And another thing . . .

San Miguel is a Spanish brewer which established a brewery in the Philippines in 1890, La Fabrica de Cerveza de San Miguel, right next door to the Spanish governor general's joint. Yes, the governor general. What is it with governors general and close proximity to grog? Wouldn't Sir John Kerr have loved the Manila posting . . .

Singha Thai Beer

Pilsener 330 ml 5.9% alc vol

This pilsener-style lager from Thailand is one of many far-eastern beers set up by the Germans years and years ago. Clear and vibrant to behold in its squat bottle, the product rings out with dry grass, drought-affected backyards, coriander gone to seed, and tapioca. The herbal perfume is followed by a sweet, middle-mouthful of coating alcohol. It's not a long, clean beer, but its flavour is full-on. This is a three-part beverage: herbal at the start, sweet in the middle and bitter on the finish.

And another thing . . .

This beer's relatively high alcohol content is a two-edged sword. One side makes it a good food beer: the alcohol sweetness copes with powerful flavours like red chilli sauce; but the 5.9% alc vol can also see you become pretty silly pretty quickly. And because you think you're just drinking beer, the silliness creeps up on you. It could be a short session.

Southwark Bitter

Lager 375ml 4.5% alc vol

On the label wrapped around its neck, Southwark Bitter proudly tells the world that it is the most bitter beer in South Australia, 'With an IBU (International Bitterness Units) of 25'. We note there is no mention of the water used. We say this because there's a whiff of finest Adelaide tap water on the nose. The pong of the estuary certainly makes for an interesting introduction. A stern, gruff bitterness lifts an otherwise flabby, malty mouthful of sweet beer. Balance isn't a strong point.

And another thing . . .

As you'll know by now, hops provide the bitterness in beer. And just as there are different varieties and applications of hops (fresh hop flowers, pellets of compacted flowers, extracted oils, dried hops, etc, etc) there are different types of bitterness: metallic, green, vegetal, rusty, tangy, zesty, astringent, unhappy, cynical . . . It's the brewer's job to decide which effect is going to best integrate with his or her brew.

48 / SESSIONAL BEERS

Stella Artois

Pilsener 330ml 5.2% alc vol

If you're sessionally drinking and want to impress, there is no better choice than Stella. You can add the Artois ('art-twah') in a poncy French accent if you want, otherwise make your desire plain by yelling STEEELLAAAH — just as Marlon Brando did in *A Streetcar Named Desire*. All the beer's ingredients are at work here. The aromatic hops deliver that first whiff of fresh hay or alfalfa; the yeast gives it some banana-cake hints. Flavourwise, there's a bit of richness from the malted barley. The bittering hops finish the drink off nicely. It's all cleverly put together.

And another thing . . .

Stella is a Belgian beer, Belgium being famous for cyclists, chocolate, monks, singer Jacques Brel and . . . um . . . beer. Mostly beer. Indeed, the Belgians drink beer like the French drink wine, and they hold it in a similarly high regard. Stella is their Foster's — mass-produced and consumed internationally, but that's where the similarities end. We know what we'd prefer to drink.

Swan Draught

Lager 375ml 4.8% alc vol

Beer labels make some strange claims. This one says: 'Traditionally brewed at 4.8% for full flavour.' But if the beer isn't light or mid-strength, 4.8% alcohol is what you'd expect, isn't it? Maybe they couldn't think of anything else to say. If we were writing the label we might mention the pale golden colour, the honey-and-hop aroma, and the fine, quenchingly bitter back palate, which all feature rather attractively in this Western Australian brew. Swan Draught, when heavily chilled, is pretty good stuff.

And another thing . . .

As well as strange claims, countless beer labels feature a picture – or artist's impression - of the brewery. And on this Swan Draught product we have what we suppose to be the Swan Brewery on the Swan River. It actually looks like a fin-de-siècle block of flats by the Seine, or a 19th-century orphanage on the Mersey. As we said, it is an artist's impression . . .

Tetley's English Ale

Brown Ale 440ml 4.4% alc vol

Tetley's smells a bit like gardening — fruits, earth, mushroom compost. It is a surprisingly exotic beer given that it's just a lad from Leeds. Maybe what we smell is its ridiculous accent. These interesting aromas come from a tight infusion of hops, yeast esters and maltings. The effect is magnificent, and makes for an integrated beer. Better still, in your mouth the slightly hard bitterness is balanced by the widget-assisted creamy texture. The only thing missing is the chip butty.

And another thing . . .

Back in Leeds the Yorkshiremen like their Tetley's to be poured from a small, tight tap. This creates a very, very fine, creamy head. This widget can seeks to emulate a barmaid's skills in producing that smooth, creamy draught-beer effect. The only trouble with widgets is that just like a barmaid after she's suffered too many leery comments they can sometimes spit the dummy. Don't open widget cans when wearing your best pair of strides.

SESSIONAL BEERS / 51

Tooheys Extra Dry

Dry Lager 345ml 5% alc vol

For once, big-company machinations have produced something worthwhile — an enjoyable, straightforward and superbly sessional beer. Amber-gold in colour, Tooheys Extra Dry — with its wheaty and yeasty smell, and a lick of malt syrup registering on your tongue before a dry and slightly dusty, beery liquid races down your throat — leaves nothing but a parching trace. There's not much body and not much structure and that means you can drink and drink and drink . . .

And another thing . . .

We've said elsewhere that beer is a natural product — a product of its environment, the available ingredients and the miracle of fermentation. Tooheys Extra Dry is more a case of the tail wagging the dog. It has been invented at every level — from the marketing meeting before it was made, right through to the manufacturing process — but it's a good sessional beer.

Tooheys New

Lager 375ml 4.6% alc vol

For mainstream, mass-market and popular Australian lager, Tooheys New is refreshingly classy. It has just a bit more going on than its interstate rivals. A little darker in colour than VB or XXXX, there's a little bit more malt action here, too. Aromas of caramel and banana come before a richer, creamier mouthful of ever so faintly bitter beer. And remember, we are talking comparatively. Once swallowed, it quickly disappears from memory in the way sessional brews are designed to.

And another thing . . .

Why is Tooheys New called 'New' when it seems to have been around for centuries? There's a very good explanation. With the broader application of temperature-controlled brewing in the 1930s came a better, more truly 'lager' style. There was another Tooheys product around — the dark one — which became known as 'Old', while the new lager was logically christened 'New'.

SESSIONAL BEERS / 53

Tooheys Red Bitter

Lager 375ml 4.2% alc vol

The best things in life are timeless. This beer describes its flavour as having 'contemporary appeal' . . . Contemporary appeal? What, like Britney Spears? The thing is you can normally buy Tooheys Red a bit cheaper than the rest of the Tooheys stable — and it tastes like it. It's a narrow, one-hit-wonder sort of beer. The main thrust is a sharp and aggressive bitter point of flavour you get just before the back of your throat. And that's pretty much it. No foreplay, and no cuddling afterwards.

And another thing . . .

Although beers such as this don't extend your brain in terms of flavour analysis, they do have a role in that magnificent, worldwide tradition of thoughtless drinking. This beer belongs to that echelon, along with such boring brews as Budweiser and Foster's. After all, if you are reasonably coordinated you don't have to think to drink.

Victoria Bitter

Lager 375ml 4.5% alc vol

VB is the most popular beer in Australia. It's consumed by the slab in every state, by loyal blokes and blokettes who swear by the green label. VB has a distinctive taste — real pubby. A yeasty beer with aromas of bittering hops rather than aromatic ones, it fills the mouth and slips down the throat with the slightest grab at the tonsils on the way, and that's pretty much We reckon this is the epitome of Australian mainstream lager — boring but consistent. Is 'the best cold beer Vic?' We don't think so.

And another thing . . .

VB's critics claim it's misnamed. It might be Victorian but it certainly isn't bitter. In fact, in bitterness units (or BUs: the way beer bitterness is measured), its CUB stable mate, Foster's, is slightly ahead, and Emu Bitter blows it out of the water completely. If you're a bitterness freak, steer clear of the mainstream and check out some India pale ales.

SESSIONAL BEERS / 55

West End Draught

Lager 375ml 4.5% alc vol

Without doubt, to Keith and Angus from Port Adelaide – drinking mates for a million years – West End Draught is a way of life. It tastes exactly as it should and exactly as it always has – of beer – but compared to other bitter lagers in Australia, this one's a simple, soapy beverage. The only thing that lifts it out of the ordinary are some awkward metallic hops that recall the draughts of yesteryear, which have long since turned up their toes. Sorry Keith and Angus.

And another thing . . .

West End Brewery is home to a spring, the water from which is greedily gathered by long-suffering, mains-water-drinking Adelaidians. This spring water is so good it seems a shame that West End can sometimes turn it into a liquid even worse than Adelaide tap water.

XXXX Bitter

Lager 375ml 4.5% alc vol

Maybe it's something cultural – we're not Queenslanders – but we just don't get XXXX. To us it's too sweet, a bit cloying, and doesn't slake. It's like a fish without a skeleton – easy to eat, with no fiddly bits, and it always tastes the same. Structureless. There's no challenge, no interest, no resistance and nothing to chew on. This beer – as a style – we consider braindead. We suppose that in brewing terms this perhaps is an achievement in itself. Indeed, you could say that all our criticisms are, to other tastes, recommendations . . .

And another thing . . .

XXXX certainly polarises people. A lot of Queenslanders loyal to their state, the maroon, and their beer, like XXXX's drinkability and effortlessness. They say how great it is in hot weather. We reckon that in hot weather a lager style needs to be a bit hoppy and tangy, and if we were making this we'd tip in another bucket of Saaz or Hallertau hops.

SESSIONAL BEERS

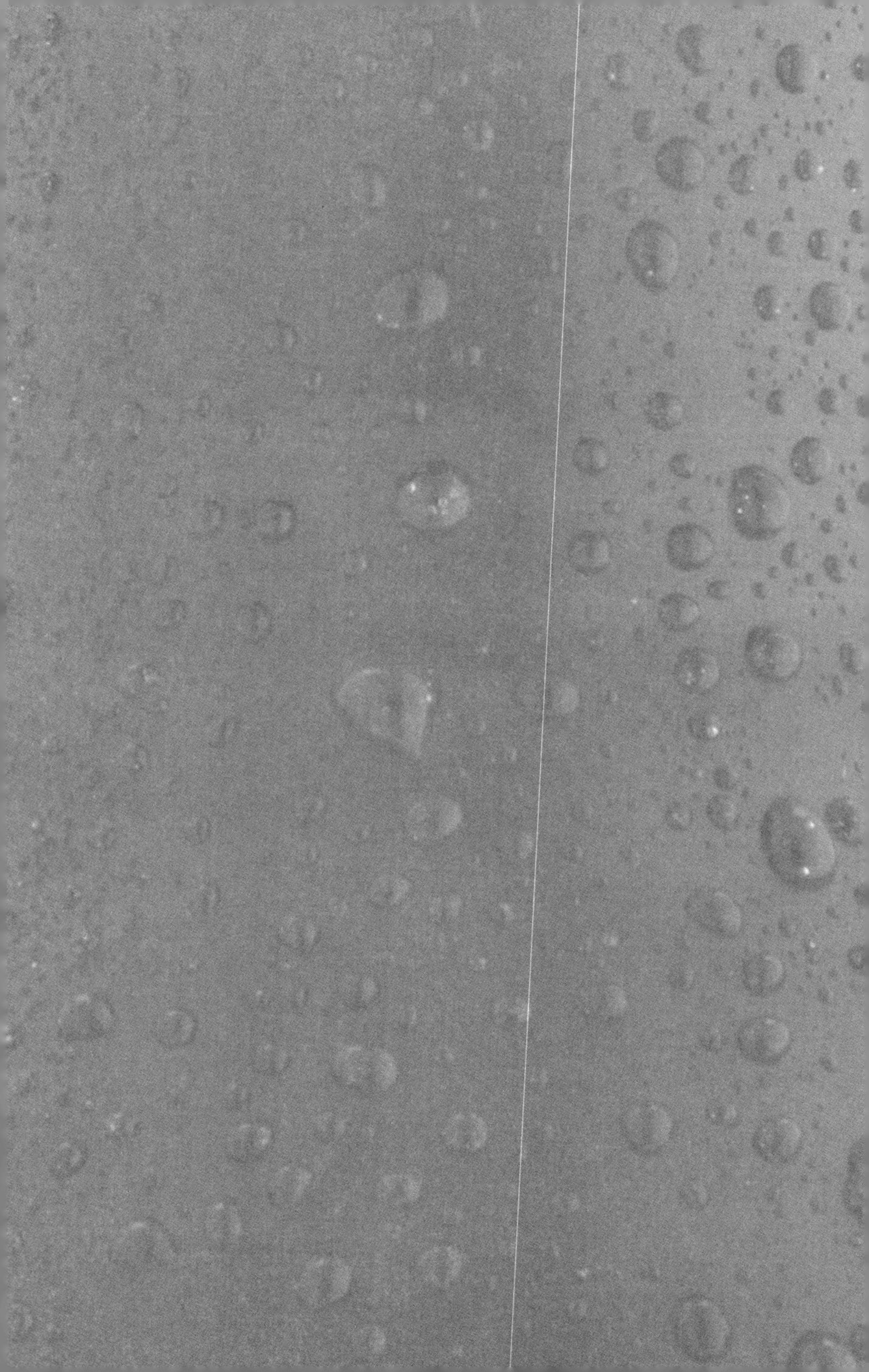

Chapter Two
Premium Beers

In this wide, amber land of lager, premium beer is a new concept. To the bloke drinking his eighteenth schooner, the idea that less is more is abhorrent – or f**king stupid, as he'd put it. The notion of paying twice as much for one beer, or only drinking (or even appreciating) a single beer after work goes against the grain of everything he's been brought up to believe – about life and beer. And when this bloke (let's call him Ken) goes home to the missus (Sharon), smelling of all that he has consumed, she can't believe there is such a thing as premium beer either . . .

But while Kens and Sharons exist in one part of the beer-drinking universe, there are Kendalls and Sharyns inhabiting another sector. They find these more expensive and more moderately consumed premium products dovetail perfectly into their credit-card-fuelled, aspirational lifestyles.

This is the world of premium beer, and it's growing. Standard workhorse beers are in a static market. Poncy premiums, both locally assembled and fully imported, exude waves of un-beer-like international sophistication, with their poofy packaging, designer bottles and posh names.

Kendall nonchalantly orders a weizenbier from the restaurant's beer list; Ken puts an empty schooner down on the bar, catches the barman's eye, perfunctorily raises one finger, and 30 seconds and three dollars later he's into his nineteenth beer.

But all hope is not lost for Ken and Kendall, Sharon and Sharyn. Their different beer-drinking galaxies are beginning to merge, for there are times for drinking sessional beers, and there are occasions that suit a more premium product.

These posh beers offer a different experience. They're

not just bottles of carbonated bitterness. Often more traditionally brewed, they use high-quality, complex and interesting ingredients, and they're designed to savour — and even to think about. Importantly, the success of premium beers is helping to lift the bar of quality across the entire beer board.

It's also providing beer drinkers with snapshots or postcards of beer flavours and styles from around the world. Kendall and Sharyn travel via their pilsener glasses to Bavaria, to little towns in Bohemia, and to Trappist abbeys in Belgium. Ken, courtesy of his nephew Miles, even reassesses his less-than-generous thoughts about the Japanese, thanks to the thirst-quenching power of a six-pack of Kirin served at a family barbecue.

This chapter contains some of Australia's best and most popular amber-coloured products, both local and imported. The best of them are very good indeed — so well made, so finely balanced, and so satisfying that one stubby can, sometimes, almost be enough . . .

Ambar Cerveza Especial

Pilsener 330ml 5.2% alc vol

There is an undeniable cultural thumbprint on the food and drink of Spain. It's as if they can't help expressing their unabashed Spanishness. This beer's no different. Much as it would probably like to be a simple sessional lager, it has a bit more than that. There's the smell of stock feed, chaff, barley in bags, and tinned molasses. The flavour in the mouth is quite rich and sweet, and a bit minerally, but a subtle dryness keeps it all in balance. The finish is satisfying and, for such a rich lager, it doesn't cloy.

And another thing . . .

One of the best things about Spain is the Spaniards' attitude towards alcohol. On all the major roadways, at nearly all the large fuel stops, not only will you find petrol bowsers and fast food but also machines dispensing 250ml beer cans. What a great place: unpasteurised driving, unpasteurised food and unpasteurised sport — bullfights.

Bitburger Premium Beer

Pilsener 330ml 4.8% alc vol

This is a bright, clear, classic-looking lager of the pilsener style. In fact, Bitburger, from Germany's Rhineland, was one of Germany's first pilseners. It has a gorgeous creamy head and its aroma offers a little bit more than many other beers of this style. Not only is there orange and lemon rind, and some floral and herb smells from the hops, but also higher, sharper bitter notes — rust, iron, slate, and metal shavings from a lathe. Indeed, there's something about Bitburger's cool, clean flavour that's reminiscent of wet steel. It has its own kind of icy, Germanic reserve. If it could speak it would speak High German — and it wouldn't speak to you.

And another thing . . .

Bitburger is best enjoyed from a wineglass. Don't be shocked. There's a lot going on aroma-wise that would be lost if you necked it straight out of the stubby. Consider investing in a few of these glasses. Your world will be changed.

Carlsberg Beer

Lager 330ml 5% alc vol

Carlsberg's clear, pale-gold colour and perfectly proportioned head impress as soon as you pour it. The aroma is fresh, with grassiness and some grain-like malty depth. In the mouth the beer is rich and round but finishes quite cleanly and assertively. There's a definite style here and it's definitely stylish. That may be because Carlsberg has its very own single-cell yeast culture: Saccharomyces Carlsbergensis. Which is a good thing to know should you ever run out of conversation.

And another thing . . .

The Carlsberg story is an amazing one. Jacob Jacobsen started Carlsberg in 1847 by pinching some bottom-fermented yeast from the Spaten Brewery in Munich. He hooned back to Copenhagen in his hotted-up four-horsepower stagecoach, keeping the yeast cool in his stovepipe hat. He subsequently became a hero and Danish TV made a 12-part mega-series about him.

64 / PREMIUM BEERS

Cascade Premium Lager

Lager 375ml 5.2% alc vol

On first sniff one of us was impressed by the hops, the other by the malt — we reckon this suggests perfect integration of those two brewing components. Rich yet pert malt versus spicy, green, herbal hops. It's the same equation inside your mouth: a friendly, smooth and round malt restrained by spicy hops. These flavours follow on to a rich midpoint in your mouth, but then it dries out to buggery — reminding us of rain on hot river stones, dew on steel, and that sort of stuff. As you've probably guessed, we like it.

And another thing . . .

Ben has a great fondness for Cascade beer. It's because of the Tassie tiger on the label. In the late 1980s there was a rumour circulating in the Dandenong Ranges of Victoria that a Tasmanian Tiger was roaming the forest — 50 years after it was supposed to have become extinct. It pretty soon was — Ben ran over the dog that was impersonating the Tasmanian Tiger a few months into the rumour. It wasn't his fault . . .

PREMIUM BEERS / 65

Coopers Sparkling Ale

Ale 375ml 5.8% alc vol

This is seriously refreshing and seriously strong ale. It has 1.3% more alcohol by volume than its green brother, the Pale Ale. Downing six of these is like drinking three bottles of white wine. It's not sessional. At the right time though, this is a fantastic beer — another one to enjoy out of a wineglass. It deserves to be treated with some respect because it's like world-champion home-brew. Rustic, cloudy, raw, with a bit of the standard Coopers sweet-and-sour action. It finishes with a strong ale's lilting unctuousness — and a ping of bitterness.

And another thing . . .

Thomas Cooper started making this beer in 1862. He was a cobbler and a Wesleyan — one of those types of Methodists who don't believe in dancing, card games or pubs. But, by a strange convolution of logic, not untypical of religious types, beer was OK.

66 / PREMIUM BEERS

Crown Lager

Lager 375ml 4.9% alc vol

Crown Lager is to premium lager what the Fairlane and Caprice are to Falcons and Commodores. You'll find them in the car parks of members-only golf clubs, and you'll find the members therein drinking Crown. It's that sort of drink. Beer drinkers need to stop and think. Just because Crown Lager is in a weird bottle, with an extravagant gold label, and has a higher price tag, doesn't mean it's better. This beer is acceptable — just. What ruins it is a cloying kind of sickly, sugary flavour that starts in the middle of your mouth and goes right through to the aftertaste. You can enjoy one glass of Crown, but two?

And another thing . . .

Crown Lager is all about unquestioned acceptance, and about not having to think about what you drink. In 21st-century Australia — so littered with ever-improving and diverse beer styles — it strikes us as a little bit odd that Crown is still king.

PREMIUM BEERS / 67

DAB Original

Pilsener 330ml 5% alc vol

DAB's a bit of a bargain. It's a fine German lager from the proud brewing city of Dortmund. There's immediate intrigue on the nose. What *is* that aroma? Grass, herbs, bark, earth, pine resin, beeswax — this is a lager in lederhosen on a nature walk. In the mouth it's quite rich to start with, then quickly dissipates — almost evaporating — leaving a long, dry, hoppy finish and aftertaste. This effect makes you want to have another glass — which is exactly what we did.

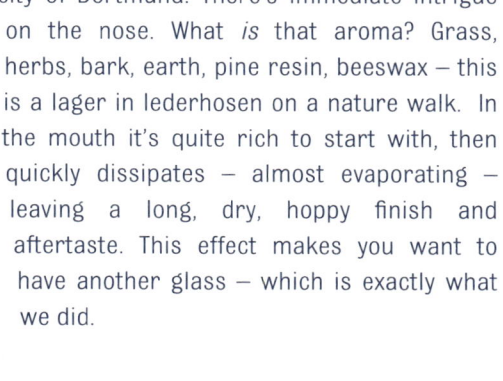

And another thing . . .

There's a simple reason this beer is called DAB. Could you ask for a Dortmunder Actien-Brauerei in a crowded, noisy pub and be understood, even if you were German? What ever you do don't ask for DUB — that stands for Dortmunder Union Brewery, and DAB and DUB are bitter rivals.

Grolsch Premium Lager

Pilsener 355ml 5% alc vol

Grolsch has a signature as soon as you sniff it. The minerally, slightly vegetal and herbal aromas get you salivating immediately. Grolsch is a remarkably fresh, refreshing beverage. The firm but clean hop smells and flavours are dry, slim and savoury. There's nothing ham-fisted or clunky about their application. Hallertau hops power this lager across the palate, leaving a trail of deliciously bitter flavour. A very good beer for hop freaks.

And another thing . . .

One way to keep beer fresh is lagering. In German, 'lager' means 'to store'. A lot of commercial lagers might only get 20 days' conditioning; Grolsch gets about 70. This makes it finer, more stable, and precludes the need for pasteurisation, a process that makes beer stable by killing it.

Hahn Premium

Lager 375ml 5% alc vol

The first thing you notice — and perhaps Hahn's most interesting characteristic — is the spicy, essential-oily and marijuana-leafy (remember the hop plant is a relative) aroma. This is the result of the brewer's late gift of hops — Hersbrucker in this case. But that's not all. This beer can handle a big late gift, thanks to its generous mouthful of malt. The two really come together at the finish when the malt's roly-polyness is knocked into shape by the hops' swathing cut. It's the epitome of a premium beer — one-and-a-half stubbies seem plenty.

And another thing . . .

When is a pilsener a lager and a lager a pilsener? Well, all pilseners fall into the broader lager family. Lager is bottom-fermented, as is pilsener, but true pilseners have a style that differentiates them from lagers. That style's accent falls strongly on hops.

Heineken Lager

Pilsener 330ml 5% alc vol

This is line and length international pilsener designed to appeal to the broadest possible beer-drinking market, which explains why it's one of the most popular beers in the world. Part of that design involves sweetness — a big dollop of malt. This makes Heineken easy to like straight off the bat (they do play cricket in the Netherlands, don't they?), but can be a bit tiring halfway through the stubby. The trick here is to drink Heineken as cold as you can.

And another thing . . .

With global success comes arrogance. In our quest to taste every beer available in Australia, we contacted Heineken's Australian office, but they wouldn't take our call. They refused to believe there was such a thing as two drinks writers putting together a beer book. They thought we were just after free beer! Can you believe it? Nice blokes like us?

PREMIUM BEERS / 71

James Boag's Premium

Pilsener 350ml 5% alc vol

Any beer addict will instantly notice the difference between James Boag's Premium and its Tasmanian counterpart, Cascade Premium, when tasting them alongside one another. James Boag's Premium is a distinctly hoppy, bitter, and, we think, more proper pilsener. It's just that no one knows what a pilsener is nowadays, so they just call it lager. This one smells of dry, dry bush: slightly coastal fringes, a hint of a blocked river channel, and the plant pigface. That aroma is its strength. In the mouth though, the beer relies more on cold temperature than brewing structure to make it through. But extra cold it's a good drink, and sessional too.

And another thing . . .

You'll have keenly noticed the rise in popularity of Tasmanian breweries. There are only two: Boag's and Cascade. The former is in the north, the latter in the south around Hobart. Water quality and the fact that Tasmania is the hop heart of Australia has a lot to do with the success of their beers.

Kingfisher Premium Lager

Lager 330ml 5% alc vol

Here's a fantastic example of an Indian beer. And when you think about it, India is a great beer country: a hot climate, thirsty population, shedloads of curries, cricket, and a British-colonial background. Kingfisher is India's number-one beer. It's a clear, pale, golden lager with a clean, white head. There's a fair bit of maltiness and body for a lager too, but it's saved from sweetness by a hit of hops that takes over in the middle of your mouth. Slightly stinky, estuary (the Ganges?) smells add to the character and interest. It made Ben think of dhal and Greg think of samosas.

And another thing . . .

Water is an important and often underrated ingredient in all beer. It makes up 95% of what you drink (the other 5% or so being alcohol). Brewers can filter and adjust the hardness and minerality of the water they use up to a point, but it will still leave its mark on the finished brew.

PREMIUM BEERS / 73

Kirin Beer

Pilsener 330ml 5% alc vol

We love a beer with a personality, and Kirin has certainly got one. It gets the beer glands excited with just a sniff. Richly golden, with a creamy head, there's a floral-herbal aroma that's quite luxurious. It smells truly 'premium'; there's nothing rustic about it. Through your mouth Kirin is tightly held together by spicy hops, leaving a clean, clear aftertaste. There's enough chewy richness on the way to sustain you, though. You won't go gay drinking this product.

And another thing . . .

This beer is named after a legendary creature that was half horse, half dragon. It appeared before the mother of Confucius, just before his birth, 2500 years ago. The sight of the Kirin is meant to herald the arrival of great men. Ipso facto: in the absence of a Kirin, we're a pretty ordinary lot . . . bring on the cold Kirin!

Labatt Blue

Pilsener 355ml 5% alc vol

The Labatt has a really distinctive taste. It's the sort of beer that once you've tried it you'll easily recognise it again without looking at the gaudy blue label. Heaps of hoppiness is expressed in quite a polite, citric way — all lemon juice and zest. There's enough body as it rolls across your tongue, but not so much that the beer flabs out. It's a racy, cool beer, perfectly designed for off-piste activities. Indeed, this beer has something of the suave French-speaking Canadian ski instructor about it, right down to the gaudy blue ski suit.

And another thing . . .

Canada is a bit of a weird beer landscape. On the one hand Canadian brewers have pioneered beer technology — ice beer (made by freezing the beer during its final lagering process) was invented north of the US border. But, then again, moronic government liquor control and intervention (stemming from the Prohibition era) has seen Canada's brewing industry hamstrung by state-run sales monopolies, high taxes and tariffs.

PREMIUM BEERS / 75

Löwenbräu Original

Pilsener 330ml 5.2% alc vol

From its umlauts to its label this beer reeks of German precision engineering. The name means 'lion beer' but there's certainly no cat's piss in this. The first thing you notice is the depth and quality of the malt, set off by aromas akin to dry grass and high-quality chaff used to feed German destriers. The flavour is balanced nicely between deep, yet reassuringly restrained malt richness, and a masculine hop bitterness. It has a dry sense of humour . . . yes, Germans can be funny.

And another thing. . .

Löwenbräu is from Munich in Bavaria — home to beer halls (Löwenbräu has the biggest), BMWs, and brass bands. It also has one of the world's most recognisable beer styles. The Munich or Münchner style is big, round and rich, but held in the taut confines of a pilsener-style lager. Their beer is less suited to quenching and more to quiet contemplation.

Nastro Azzurro

Pilsener 330ml 5.2% alc vol

Nastro Azzurro has a distinctive hoppiness, as if the brewers use a variety of hops that no one else does. It has the smell of brand-new tennis shoes (Dunlop Volleys) and red clay, or entoutcas. The malt has a honey aroma, as if the honey has come from bees feeding on flowering herbs. That sweetness continues in the mouth but it's countered by quenching, astringent, steely hops. The body of the beer dissipates quickly. Though powerfully flavoured, it doesn't seem to weigh you down.

And another thing . . .

When you think of Italy, from whence this beer comes (Nastro Azzurro means Blue Ribbon, by the way), you think of wine. Fair enough. Up until the 1960s Italians drank less than three litres of beer per capita per annum. Compare that to Australian beer consumption at roughly the same time: 140 litres per capita. Put this way, it makes Nastro Azzurro's quality quite an achievement.

PREMIUM BEERS / 77

Paulaner Original Müncher

Pilsener 330ml 4.5% alc vol

The colour of this beer is the best: happy, golden yellow. It looks sun-kissed. The aroma is sweet with honey, extract of malt, honeysuckle, and a hint of lavender. This fine lager lies around in your mouth as if luxuriating on cushions, before making a quick exit. It's not a quenching beer and is best suited to cool-climate drinking — that weekend you have away at the snow with Hildegarde, the German hydrofoil pilot.

And another thing . . .

This German beer is made using quite a few traditional techniques, one of which is krausening, a natural way to carbonate beer. After the beer is made it goes into a lagering tank for conditioning, or carbonation. A dose of raw, unfermented malt sugar is added; in the tank the malt sugar turns into the soft, pillowy bubbles that bead through your beer glass as you drink it. This krausening process is the same as a home-brewer adding a teaspoon of sugar to the bottle before the crown seal goes on.

Samuel Adams Boston Lager

Lager 355ml 4.8% alc vol

This lager has the copper colour of a light beer, but don't be fooled by that; it packs a powerful hop punch. If you think all American beers are tasteless, this will definitely change your mind. What's more, if you're into hard-core, medicinal, herbal hop grip, you're going to love Samuel Adams even more. The aroma is completely dominated by dried hops. The rather rich, nutty palate is held in check by the hops, and the everlasting length is, likewise, attributable to the heavy-handed hopping. Given all that, we like it. A lot.

And another thing...

First brewed in 1984, this lager uses caramel malt, hence the darker colour and nutty flavour, but it gets its most distinctive flavour from a brewing technique known as dry hopping. Hallertau, Mittelfrueh, Tettnang and Tettnanger hops are added when the beer has finished fermenting, giving it that individual aroma and tang. Hops rock.

Southwark Premium Lager

Lager 375ml 5.2% alc vol

The hopping of beer is a delicate art. Like cooking with chilli it's important when you add it, how you add it, and in what quantity. Chop up chillies and chuck them in the stir-fry at the last minute and the dish will be out of balance – talk about a burning ring of fire. De-seed them, paste them and infuse them into the dish from the very beginning and you'll get a better effect. This Southwark is a hastily made stir-fry. The hops aren't integrated and they're a bit on the steely-rusty side. You drink it because it's beer and you're thirsty. Once again, a beer-like beer.

And another thing . . .

Making beer is a lot like cooking – advanced cooking. And while making beer might be easy, it's not simple. Thousands of disgusting home-brews attests to that. Brewing has a lot of different phases; it's probably more akin to cordon bleu cooking than whipping up a stir-fry.

Steinlager

Pilsener 330ml 5% alc vol

There's no doubt that for an otherwise fairly standard premium brew, Steinlager has some distinctiveness — and two tricks up its sleeve. The first is an attractively subdued background of honeyed malt aroma that leads you on, playing hard to get. In your mouth this malt hides behind every hop corner. The second is that the hops in this beer really linger, like a herbal, bitter mouthwash. In many ways New Zealand's South Island is perfect for hop growing and Steinlager benefits from it.

And another thing . . .

Steinlager hit the international headlines and went apeshit in 1985 when it won an international lager award, beating the world's best. This was the equivalent to New Zealand winning the America's Cup, the All Blacks winning the Rugby World Cup, or their cricket team drawing a test series with Australia. The fuss about Steinlager has subdued, but the beer is still a champion.

Tiger Beer

Lager 330ml 5% alc vol

If you can't find something to like in Tiger, you're hard to please. It's got everything a good lager should have: an attractive golden colour, a good head, and a crisp, clean carry. Furthermore, what body and maltiness the beer has is held in a crisp, hoppy envelope as it passes from lips to throat. It's this quality that makes it so refreshing. Indeed, this beer could well be in Chapter One. It is both sessional and satisfying. In short, it rocks.

And another thing . . .

We've described the hops here as crisp and refreshing as opposed to dry and gruff. There are many varieties of hops and they are used at different times in the brewing process. Some are added early; some are added late. Their accent can fall on different parts of the beer: its structure, its aroma, its finish. Hops are the signature of every beer and Tiger signs off very nicely.

Tsingtao Beer

Pilsener 330ml 4.3% alc vol

You'd expect a beer from China to be different, and Tsingtao is. No, it's not made from ground chicken feet or dried tiger penis. It still uses the traditional big three ingredients: hops, malt and water. It does, however, have German ancestry (Germans set up the brewery in the 19th century), which explains Tsing's unabashed pilsener flavour. But it has something more exotic, too: the hops have a minerally, drying texture which aid the beer's quenchability. And there's a slight saltiness also registering — which makes it good with prawn gow gee.

And another thing. . .

Every time we have a yum cha business lunch the Tsingtao tastes different, and it's not the yum cha's fault — nor the business's. Tsingtao is notoriously inconsistent — in malt, hopping and freshness. It's usually there or thereabouts, but one bottle can be OK, another really good. But bottle variation exists in many things — beer, wine, Coca Cola . . .

PREMIUM BEERS / 83

Tuborg Gold Label

Pilsener 330ml 5.5% alc vol

There's a bit more gold about the colour of this gold-label Tuborg than most of the beers in this chapter. The aroma is one of hop oil, resin and clothes in cupboards. (Actually, the concentrated resinous smells reminded one of us of hashish. We're just not saying which one of us.) There's nothing to find fault with in the consistency of the bubble, in the way the flavours run through the mouth, or in the spicy bitterness with which it finishes. This beer deserves its gold label.

And another thing . . .

Local knowledge is always interesting. Carlsberg might be Denmark's international star, sold in 150 countries and brewed in more than 40, but Tuborg is what the Danes actually love to drink — and how. We reckon this is because of Tuborg's stronger hop accent. Hops equal bitterness, and advanced beer drinkers like bitterness. Or maybe it's that aroma of hashish . . .

84 / PREMIUM BEERS

Warsteiner

Pilsener style 330ml 4.8% alc vol

Warsteiner tastes serious and sounds serious. *Vvah-shtinah*. But the German language is always a bit menacing. (We're actually writing this down with a *Kugelschreiber* – a pen.) The Warsteiner aroma is not shy. It's a balance of bitter, zesty hops and fruity yeast-derived enzymes. There's a malty, caramelised richness and a hint of wild honey. But there are no confectionery notes. The effect is very satisfying and just as you think the last note of the Warsteiner artillery has sounded, there's a herbal, bitter reprise right at the end. It's full-flavoured and it's grouse.

And another thing . . .

Beer and food. No, this does not mean bar snacks like chips and nuts. This beer deserves something a bit more complicated. Its balanced bitterness and full flavour would help you fight through the fat and flavour of a couple of spicy bratwurst sausages, pickled ox tongue, or your own weight in smoked salmon. Polski ogorki, horseradish, capers, raw onion . . .

PREMIUM BEERS / 85

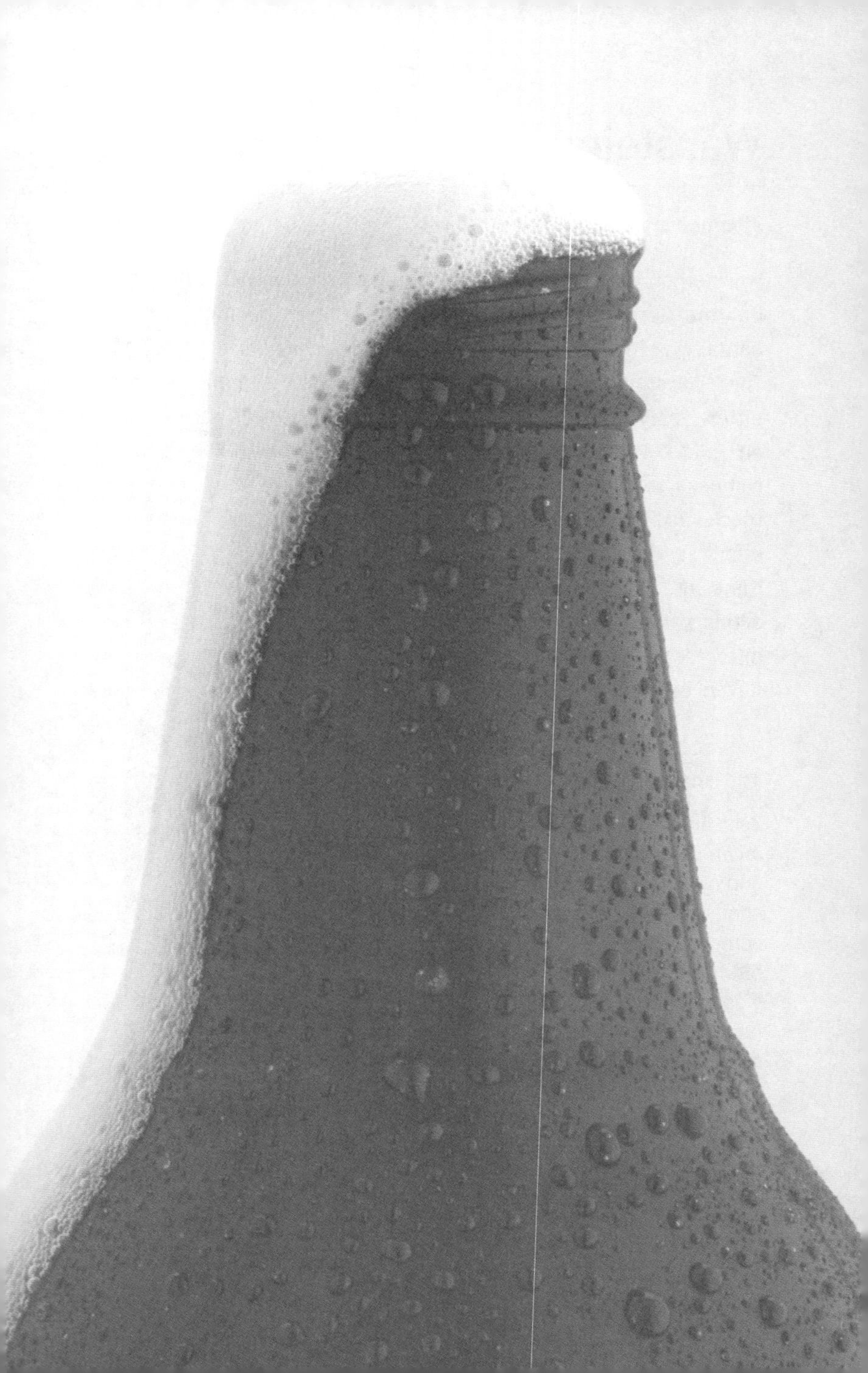

Chapter Three
Boutique Beers

Boutique beers are not just for hairdressers. Nor are they made in hairdressing salons. They're characterful beers that are created in small volumes. They sit somewhere between home-brew and the mega-multinational beer conglomerates – a pretty good place to be.

Boutique beers are a bit like independently produced records. They're not for every taste, but they do have a taste. It's a taste that has its own personality, whether you like that personality or not. Yet sometimes, boutique beers can have all the – how should we put it? – foibles of your mate Derek's most interesting home-brew. You know, the one that sent everyone to hospital. The one that looked like paint, smelt like paint, and eventually applied itself (by an unconventional spray-on method) to the inside walls of the smallest room in the house.

Boutique breweries are often termed micro-breweries – and the word 'micro' is used proudly. After all, boutique brewers are using exactly the same ingredients and following the same sorts of recipes as the big boys, the difference being that they have the latitude to pursue some of their more bizarre boutique beer bents. The boutique brewer is part alchemist, part cook, part Dr Frankenstein and part creative genius.

A boutique brewer will often start his or her career by turning perfectly good home-brew kits into bottled drain cleaner. But they're on a mission and, with an application to duty fuelled by some of the world's best beer (and a hatred for the mundane), their garages become bottling lines and the bungalow a micro-brewery. Soon they've got a loyal, if illegal, following. Soon thereafter they have a liquor licence and a business loan. Too cool inner-city pubs fight for their Poofters Pilsener, Leg Opener Lager, and Fat Arse Ale.

Next, a lifestyle journalist from one of Australia's 783 glossy food and wine magazines discovers them. In a 12-page colour lift-out, Leg Opener Lager and Fat Arse Ale are elaborately matched to a leading chef's signature dishes. Before they know it, the boutique brewer has Lion Nathan and CUB knocking on the door. They sell their garage brewery for $28 million.

Or at least that's the dream.

The thing to remember about boutique beers is that they are moving targets. From one batch to the next there can be minor differences. Like singer-songwriters with songs, they don't do it the same way twice. They're happy to sacrifice continuity of flavour for new, more interesting flavours. That's what makes for different and potentially more exciting beers. Generally speaking, boutique beers are worth thinking about.

Little Creatures Pale Ale

Pale Ale 330ml 5.2% alc vol

There's something about cloudy, richly golden beers that seems healthy and organic — and a little suspicious — all at the same time. But this is no rustic home-brew; it's fresh and exotic. Smells of rosewater, geraniums and citrus peel remind us more of aromatic white wines than they do of beer. But there's nothing poofy about this beer's palate. It's as bitter as a mouthful of galvanised nails. It needs food. Thai fish cakes, coconut cream, fluffy rice . . .

And another thing . . .

Do beer names mean anything? For instance, what happens when you drink Carlton Cold unrefrigerated? What happens to a young, able-bodied person when they drink Invalid Stout? Thank goodness Little Creatures is aptly named — after all those little creatures (the micro-biowhatsits — like yeast, enzymes and proteins) swimming around in the additive and preservative-free liquid environment.

Little Creatures Rogers' Beer

Brown Ale 330ml 3.8% alc vol

This beer is more amber than brown, and more hoppy and citrussy than a lot of traditional English ales. That's part of the Little Creatures mantra: hops, hops, and more hops. Its vibrant, reddish amber colour suits its body and texture; the beer slips through your mouth with enough to chew on, but no flab. There's balance. The hop bitterness is expressed more in a sharp and spiky way than in a gruff and parching manner. It finishes without a fight, although there's just a dab of caramel and a twist of lemon that reminds you of the start.

And another thing . . .

For many dedicated beer drinkers, having a beer named after them would be the greatest honour. As knighthoods have been devalued and all the streets have been named, beer labels are one of the last places where truly great Australians can be made immortal. This beer was named after a couple of Rogers.

Matilda Bay Premium

Pilsener 345ml 4.9% alc vol

There's a bit of the Swan River at low tide about this beer. It's stinky and home-made smelling, yet in a natural way. There's also a distant hop aroma — and boy, do these hops take over once the beer is past your lips. They're rustic, horny-handed hops; they carry the moussy malt and help to effervesce it before realising their own astringent crescendo. Another beer for hop addicts, and Greg reckons it would be a great drink heavily chilled on a stinking hot day.

And another thing . . .

Matilda Bay came out of the opulent 1980s micro-brewery ridiculousness. Most of those breweries imploded and sold off their lauter tuns. Some stuck it out, continuing to make good beer and eventually reaping the rewards. They were bought out by the big breweries (making shitloads of cash), but were allowed to continue making beer in their own style. In a beer world with plenty of diversity but not much personality, these beers rock.

Mountain Goat Hightail Ale

Brown Ale 330ml 4.5% alc vol

Here's a malty ale with some bottle condition. There's plenty going on in the aroma. We smell a certain type of salami (Milanese or Sopressa), earthiness, and green herbs. The cloudy, rich liquid registers more luxurious caramelised flavours on your tongue but as it edges towards sweetness it checks itself and the flavour goes back to more savoury things: gravy, and Vegemite on toast. Like a lot of ales it finishes with an inert, almost silent thud — but that's ale and that's why they drink them in pints.

And another thing . . .

Bottle conditioning. In the stubby of Hightail we tried there was a solid deposit of dead yeast cells and sediment. It's a signature of quality. After the beer is bottled, the dying yeast cells fall through the solution as the stubby lies on its side. Yet even when they're dead, their work isn't done; their remains add flavour and complexity to the ale.

BOUTIQUE BEERS / 93

Mountain Goat India Pale Ale

Pale Ale 330ml 5% alc vol

This is exactly what you're looking for in a boutique ale. With regard to brewing quality, it crosses the t's and dots i's, but, in addition, it has the boutique bonus: character and individuality — and a little bit of funk. Cloudy and copper-bronze in colour, it's probably darker than most true pale ales. The smell (sharp, aromatic, hop-oily) and the taste (round, a little rich and roasted, but kept taut and streamlined thanks to the extra hops) deliver the classic IPA (India Pale Ale) friendly punch.

And another thing . . .

This beer claims to be Australia's first 100% organic beer. It even says on the label that it's certified as an organic processor by the BFA, the Biodynamic Federation of Australia. It makes you ask the question, who needs genetic modification when organic beers can taste so good?

Mountain Goat Pale Ale

Pale Ale 330ml 4.5% alc vol

Although the head of this dirty-amber-coloured ale resembles washing-up water, when you lift the beer to your nose it's aromatic. What's more, we reckon this beer is a bit of a health tonic: lemon thyme, essential oils, spice, honeycomb . . . The flavour combines a richness with a surrounding clean astringency. Its texture is that of a true ale: low carbonation and fizz, and easy and soft as it goes down. The finish is really hoppy (Hallertau hops in this case), and it's a really good drink to kick off the day.

And another thing . . .

In the review above we mentioned beer's texture: ales and lagers have different ones. Lagers are more pert, lively, fluffy and effervescent in texture. On the other hand, the texture of ales is more staid, soft, and less like a fizzy drink. Each suit different drinking occasions, moods or thirst.

Oakbank Beer

Ale 375ml 4.9% alc vol

Here's an ale at the opulent, in-yer-face end of the beer stick. It's very rich and sweet, smelling of caramels and rum-and-raisin ice cream. It's creamy and overtly malty with all the flavour falling on the tip of your tongue. From there it dissipates with a soft, cloying finish — helped out a bit by some residual bitterness. This is the antithesis of a sessional beer. One of these is plenty.

And another thing . . .

This beer is classed traditionally as a 'dinner ale', which makes you wonder what people ate back in the olden days. Heavily corned mutton? Cauliflower with white sauce? Beetroot? Meat loaf? Tongue? Pelican? We actually don't think this is a good beer with food. Its luscious maltiness would struggle to find a partner in any of the foods we eat today.

Redback Original

Wheat Beer 345ml 4.7% alc vol

With wheat beer's characteristic aroma of chaff and lemon rind, this fairly drinkable Redback is far from poisonous. Indeed, if a more toxic wheat beer has bitten you, this one might just prove to be the antivenene. It's very line and length; Redback isn't trying to be too funky. Those wheat and citrus smells also contain a touch of orange — those old ones lying around in the fruit bowl. The flavour has the directness of classic wheat beers and stays fairly taut. The texture is more fine than grainy. Jam a slice of lemon in the top and you're in wheat-beer heaven.

And another thing . . .

Wheat beers are in a class of their own, but are made like ales — that is, top fermented. Using wheat as the starch gives the brewer an entirely new spectrum of flavours to play with, not to mention textures. Wheat beers are a bit of an acquired taste. Don't expect VB. And don't be too dismissive; chill it down and try to understand it as you would a very beautiful foreign girl . . .

BOUTIQUE BEERS / 97

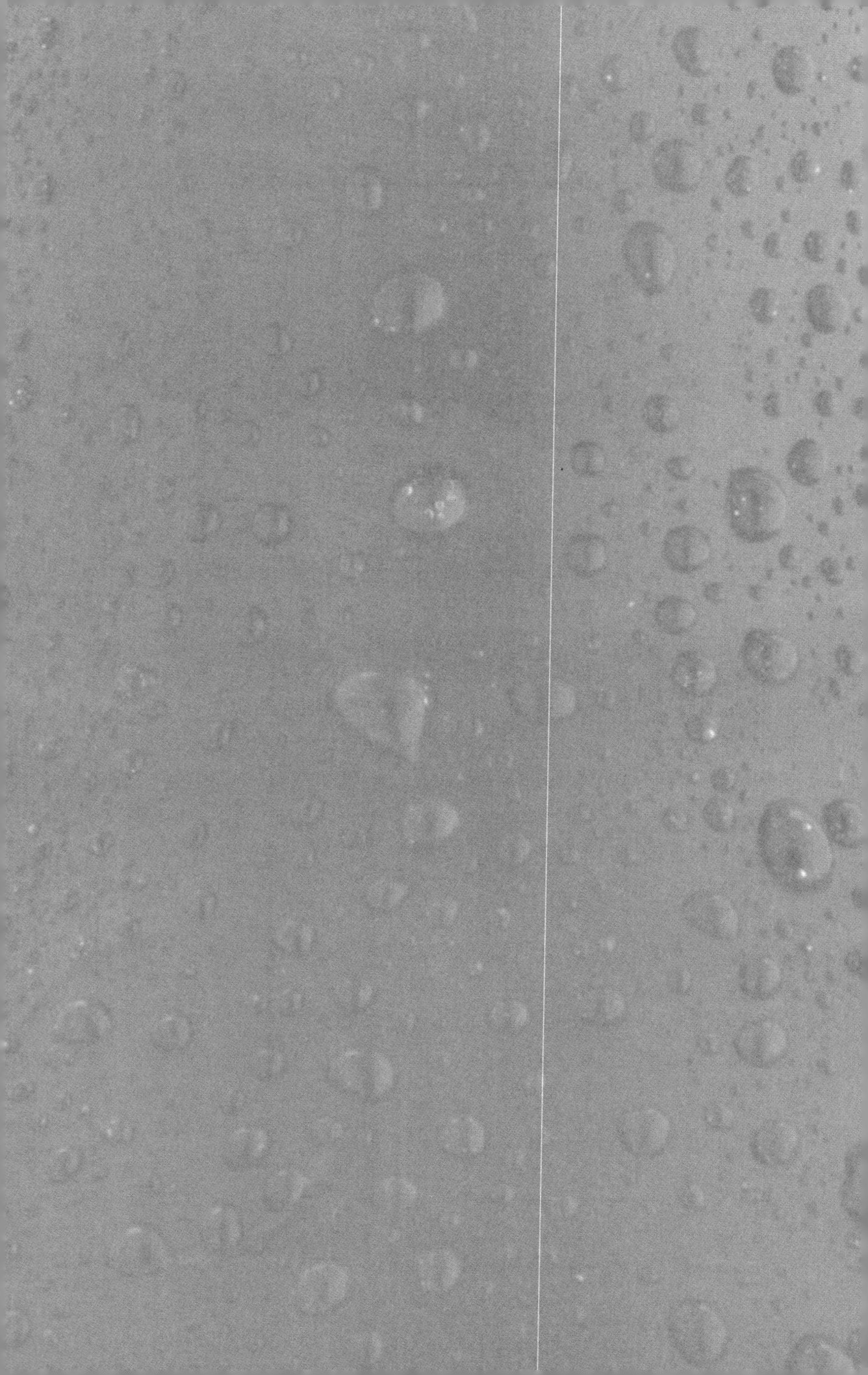

Chapter Four
Heavy Beers

It's easy to ignore the dark side of beer's personality and just think of light, cute, frothy lagers. But that would be a mistake, for some of ale's most interesting children are on the weighty side.

But if you've never developed a taste for ale's fatter kids, it's not your fault. In Australia we are taught from birth by beer companies, our parents, John Mellion, and our harsh, hot climate that a 'hard-earned thirst needs a big cold beer'. We are brainwashed into thinking that beer drinking is all about quenching and nothing else. Even when we're drinking sessionally and up to our umpteenth beer, we are still 'quenching a thirst' (a thirst for *what* is never actually discussed). To actually drink a big black beer really slowly is something that is only just starting to happen in gauche Irish theme pubs and Belgian beer cafes. But sipping a highly flavoured ale is something Australians don't do enough of. There's a whole segment of beer drinking we're missing out on. Once again, it's the fault of wine. In non-wine-producing countries such as Belgium, Britain and Germany, big heavy beers take the place of wine. They get cellared, sniffed, matched with food and discussed with the same 'passion' and pretension. Beer tossers are as common in those countries as wine tossers are over here. It's all very well to dwell over a double-bock or Trappist brew for a while, but don't take it too far.

The important thing is not to be racist when it comes to dark beers so that you just think of them as being black or brown or dusky coloured. You don't understand them so you don't like them. But there's more to the darker, heavy beers than just colour and it is a crime, if not against humanity then at least against beer, if you fail to apply yourself to them.

It is true that dark, heavy beers are made differently from their paler brothers. The dark ones are typified by heavily roasted malts, giving chocolate, coffee, liquorice, toffee, caramel, and earthy aromas and flavours to the brew. But even more important than colour is body. These dark ales have entirely different physiques to the lithe lagers. Top-fermentation at warmer temperatures makes for a more hulking, heavily built, and slow — but, in his own way, effective — sort of fellow.

Indeed, if we were Sir David Attenborough, we'd breathlessly pronounce stouts to be like 'mighty, lurching walruses barking hoarsely as they besport themselves awkwardly on wave-crashed rocks'. Still in Attenborough mode, we might liken a lager to 'a baby female fairy penguin tripping and hopping delicately and playfully from the sand into the cold, clean, frothy ocean's edge'. Both the walrus and the penguin are creatures of the sea, just as stouts and lagers are both beers. To behold, both look entirely different, but once under water (or inside your mouth) they move with elegance and ease down into the murky depths below.

There is, of course, not just one type of walrus; heavy beers come in lots of different shapes and forms. From the unctuous, alcoholic amber ales, through to brown ales and dark ales, to porter, and then on to stouts, it's a diverse genus in which the colour gets darker — and the winter stews start to beckon.

As that suggests, the winter months or cooler climes are the best times and places to drink heavy, dark beers: the alcohol warms, the ale's body comforts, and the dark, roasted malt sustains. Warmth, comfort, sustenance — it's no mistake that Guinness is from Ireland.

One more thing to note well is the way many dark beers

don't taste as good in the can or the stubby as from the pub. Dark, heavy beers are best when they're cask-conditioned and hand-pumped, but unfortunately this is a hard thing to replicate thousands of kilometres away from their source. Widget cans (with the little plastic nitrogen-dispensing ball inside) do go some of the way towards mimicking the smooth, creamy draught action of a hand-pumped beer but, as always, there's nothing like the real thing — that's why people travel . . .

Beamish Genuine Irish Stout

Stout 500ml 4.2% alc vol

Well at least with a can of Beamish you get 500ml. Otherwise, this very straightforward stout is a little bit lacking. After all, when it comes to drinking stout, we figure you either go hard or go home. You're not just doing it to be fashionable, or are you? This widget-charged product is like a stout that's been neutered. It's cute to look at, it's creamy and it sort of purrs through your mouth, but there's no bite — except maybe that flavour of badly made coffee that hangs around after you swallow it.

And another thing . . .

This is a true Irish story. There was a pub in Cork that served its own stout. After a while, it began to get a bit popular. Rowan, Fergal and Michael would go there and drink pints of the stuff. Soon they began to put on weight — became a bit beamish as they say in Cork. That's how this stout got its name.

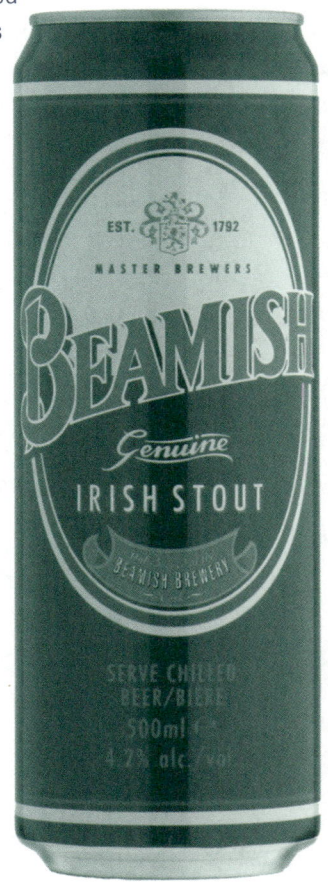

HEAVY BEERS / 103

Castlemaine Carbine Stout

Stout 375ml 5.1% alc vol

If you love iced coffee you'll particularly enjoy the aroma of this stout. If you hate iced coffee you'll detest it. It has the same heavy, milky palate, with an iced-coffee–confectionery finish. There's simply not enough structure, no drying hop bitterness at the finish. The nicest thing we can find to say about it is that it has a great label. But we wouldn't recommend it to anyone to drink.

And another thing . . .

The alcoholic-beverage industry worldwide is obsessed with what is known as 'importing heritage value'. That is, if you've got a product that is a bit dead in the water, attach to it a bit of historic cachet. Carbine was a champion racehorse. No one knows if it drank stout or not . . .

Coopers Best Extra Stout

Stout 375ml 6.3% alc vol

This is better than a poke in the eye with a burnt stick. In fact, there's a bit of the burnt stick about it — a burnt green stick. There's also a bit of cooking chocolate, the bits scraped from the bottom of the roasting pan, old chests of drawers, brake fluid and iced coffee. Around the edges, it takes no prisoners. It's firm and aggressive, but it does have a smooth middle ground, full of coffee and cream. This is a stout that doesn't muck around.

And another thing . . .

Fanatics of this stout like to lie it on its side and leave it in a dark, cool spot for a few years. The bottle still contains yeast cells, which (deceased though they are) continue to interact with the beer, making for a smoother and slightly more complex beverage. It's great stuff.

Coopers Special Old Stout

Stout 375ml 6.8% alc vol

What sets this stout apart from its peers is the integration of its flavours. The coffee, the chocolate, and the et cetera aren't in your face. It's a self-assured beer. It doesn't shout its CV out at you like some American time-and-motion management guru; it simply introduces itself, a bit like an elderly Australian gentleman. Indeed, that analogy is very true. All the work has been done in this beer before you drink it. Long top-fermentation and lengthy conditioning equates to a smooth, complex stout.

And another thing . . .

Apparently this stout came about not through a new product meeting at the Cooper's family dinner table but in response to the fact that devotees of Coopers Best Extra Stout (see page 105) were cellaring it. If you don't drink this particular beer fresh it doesn't matter; you can cellar it, and it can get better.

106 / HEAVY BEERS

Guinness Draught

Stout 440ml 4.2% alc vol

Guinness is an icon, a drink loved by millions. So brilliant is Guinness in Ireland that a demand exists to take it all around the world. But from a technical point of view this is impossible. At home it's an unpasteurised miracle; exported it's an automaton. With smells of iced coffee and liquorice, it unfortunately dissipates and disappoints in the mouth. Its bitterness somehow cloys rather than cleans. Sorry.

And another thing . . .

The Guinness pictured here is the very popular widget can. We tried not only the imported can, but the imported widget stubby and also the 800ml bottle brewed locally under licence. All were completely different — the 800ml bottle particularly so. It had 6% alcohol. The moral: Guinness ain't Guinness . . .

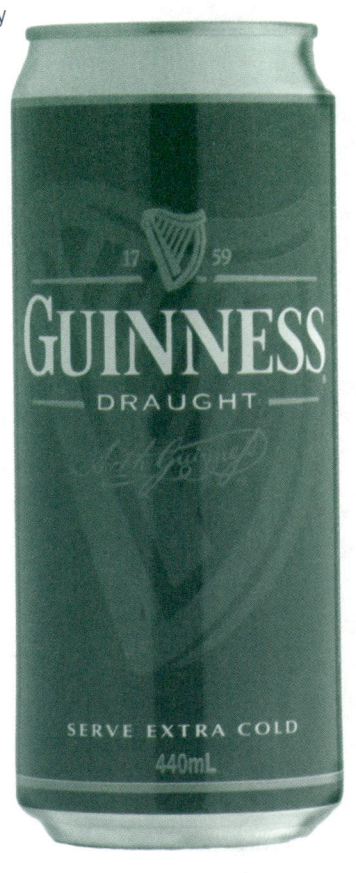

James Squire Original Amber Ale

Ale 345ml 5% alc vol

Ben: 'That's not bad.' Greg: 'Actually, that's quite good.' This accurately named Original Amber Ale surprised us. There's heaps to smell and savour, including beeswax, shellac and heavily polished, well-kept, old furniture. With a powerful flavour of intense and almost concentrated maltiness, it leaves the palate gently and without a fuss, tailing off with a hint of cinnamon teacake. It's almost a shock to discover it's only 5% alcohol. Is the number on the label a typo?

And another thing . . .

How do you use a beer like this? For a start — and we know this sounds a bit gay — you and your mate should share this bottle of beer, drinking it from a couple of tulip-shaped wineglasses. The glasses will funnel the beer's interesting and worthwhile aromas up into your nose, helping you appreciate the complexity we mentioned. You might even like to put on an old Barbra Streisand record . . .

James Squire India Pale Ale

Pale Ale 345ml 5.6% alc vol

This is the antithesis of sessional beer. One is definitely enough. But that's not a criticism, it's a compliment. It's light copper in colour, and the rich, characterful and slightly intriguing malt body is tautened by the iron grip of English Fuggles hops. It actually smells cool, like ozone gas or a new beer fridge. The finish is full of minerals and earth, and limestone. It leaves your mouth and you somehow feel healthier and improved.

And another thing . . .

India Pale Ale, or IPA as it's called in the business, came about when the Poms owned India. They wanted beer and so had it shipped over from England. What with the voyage and the heat and everything the beer was rotten by the time it got to Calcutta. To keep it stable they added more hops (remember they're a preservative) and more alcohol. IPA was born.

James Squire Porter

Dark Ale 345ml 5% alc vol

Power-packed, gamut-running and in no way quietly spoken, here is a dark ale — or porter — that will interest if not intrigue in terms of its broad spectrum of flavours. Everything from coffee, toffee, molasses, chocolate ice cream, raisins, stewed prunes, coffee grounds and even a bit of iced coffee ring out. Sip it slowly and let it warm up a little in the glass and you won't need anything else.

And another thing . . .

There's a push in Australia now to make beer more sophisticated by aligning certain beer styles with certain foods — or dishes, as they are known. Bullshit. One may choose to enjoy a pecan chocolate tart with one's porter, but, then again, one may prefer a simple bag of crisps. It's a matter of personal choice.

Leffe Radieuse

Brown Ale 330ml 8.2%

Here's a full-on, sermonic, lectern-pounding, fire-and-brimstone brew from our very good friends at the Abbaye de Leffe in Belgium. Leffe Radieuse is a toffee-coloured brown ale with the ripe-fruit and sweet-malt volume knobs turned all the way to 11. This is not everyone's brand of religion, but it will win its fair share of converts. Its weight and texture are luxuriant and almost seductive, enveloping and swamping the senses.

And another thing . . .

8.2% alcohol. Is this wine or beer? Most of us think of beer as being around 4 or 5%, not double that. A higher alcohol level can be achieved through such processes as double-malting (malt is the fuel that provides alcohol), adding sugar (another fuel for alcohol production), and wort reduction through boiling (just like reducing a sauce on top of the stove).

Paulaner Salvator

Bock 330ml 7.5% alc vol

Bocks are sweet, alcoholic lagers whose names usually end in 'tor'. This Salvator (salvator means saviour) is actually a doppel-bock, so it's even stronger than a bock. It has a reddish mahogany colour and smells like your mum's Christmas cake and Grandma's furniture. The body of the beer lounges on your tongue with considerable weight. Three types of malt are used in its production, but only Hallertau hops are included. They do a great job of rescuing this beer from red-faced portliness; they dry your mouth out and keep it relatively fresh after each sip.

And another thing . . .

Sipping is the key to appreciating Salvator. Knock back a couple of stubbies of this after work and you'll need your own Salvator to drive you home, or pour you into the train. It's a cold-winter's-night, wineglass, wood-fire, sit-down-and-have-a-quiet-chat sort of beer.

Sheaf Stout

Stout 375ml 5.7% alc vol

Old ashtrays, bar towels, beer-soaked furniture, nicotine-stained light fittings — we can imagine the pub, and this beer smells like it belongs there. It's a one-dimensional mouthful of stout. The only thing that lifts it is an over-the-top metallic clang of hops right at the back. This keeps ringing long after you swallow it, like a phone that no one will answer . . .

And another thing . . .

There are Sheaf Stout drinkers out there who will, no doubt, be offended by what we've said. But that's the way we see — or taste — it. If you are a Sheaf Stout drinker, don't despair. There are good reasons why you like Sheaf Stout. Empirical studies have proven that beer loyalty has nothing to do with taste — it's all about myth, legend and blind parochialism.

Southwark Old Stout

Stout 375ml 7.4% alc vol

Greg really enjoyed his first sip of this stout, but it may have been the alcohol talking. Concentrated, a little syrupy, and certainly well-bittered, this stout is — make no mistake about it — powered by alcohol. But there's nothing wrong with that. Alcohol tracks flavour, so you get plenty of stout's coffee and bitter dark chocolate flavours here, along with a bit of meatiness and some Vegemite. Sip this beer on a dark and stormy night; convince your lover/significant other to share a stubby with you, and the world will be your oyster.

And another thing . . .

Oysters and stout? The countries that invented the bizarre practice of consuming them together do not make wine. A freshly shucked oyster is perfect with good, dry white wine and has no relationship with the roasted flavours of stout — coffee, chocolate, etc. But then again, there is such a thing as Oyster Kilpatrick.

Tooheys Old

Dark Ale 375ml 4.4% alc vol

The colour of Tooheys Old leads you to expect that it's going to be heavier and stronger than it actually is, but with a really nice, fluffy, creamy head, the texture of the beer is surprisingly crisp and clean. It's not at the coffee-and-cocoa end of the dark-beer spectrum; in fact, this dark beer is almost sessional. It finishes crisp and clean, with a good whack of bitterness that's ever so slightly astringent. Good for quenching a thirst on a cold day.

And another thing . . .

Tooheys Old is an archaeological remnant of Australia's brewing past. It has used the same top-fermenting yeast ever since it first became available on tap in 1869. It must have been a good strain of yeast because in Sydney's stinking hot summers, without refrigeration top-fermented lagers would have gone absolutely stupid. Indeed, at that time many ales were known for their laxative effect.

HEAVY BEERS

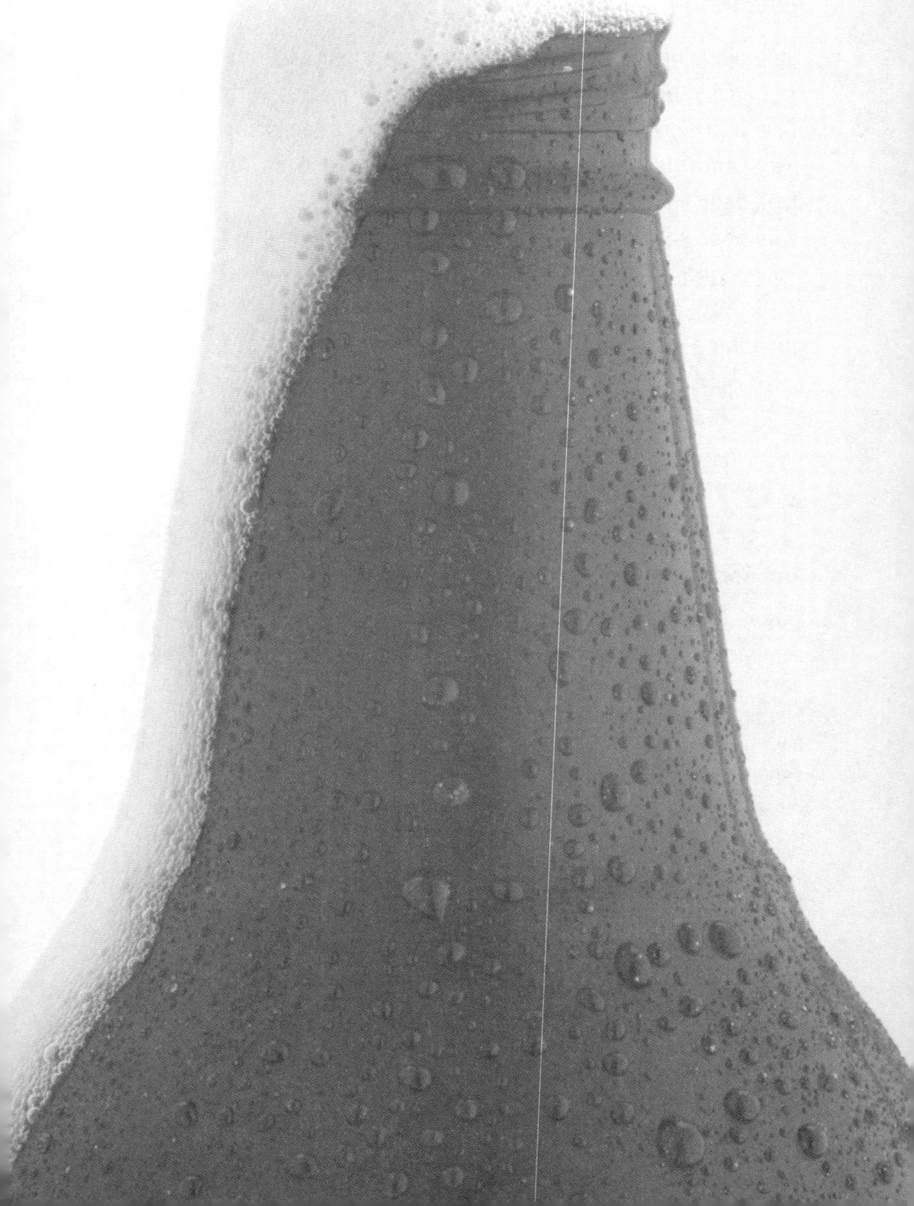

Chapter Five
Light Beers

Once upon a time in a country called Australia the people therein made cups of tea, were unaware of cholesterol, didn't have seat belts in their Holdens, and drank full-strength beer before letting the Holden drive them home.

Thank goodness those days are gone . . .

In the here and now of contemporary Australia we drink chardonnay, fret about fat, strap ourselves into Magnas and Lantras, and enjoy the miracle of 'lite'. We can drink beer and not get pissed. We can quench our thirsts and honour a 5000-year human tradition — and still find our way back to the cave . . .

But why don't we drink more light beer? There are psychological and gustatory answers to this question. Light beer is thin and pissy; ipso facto, light-beer drinkers are pooftahs — simple Australian logic.

As for light beer's taste, well, there is a very good reason why, until the invention of drink driving, there was no such thing as 'lite'. Beer is 4 to 6% alcohol by volume because conventional brewing yeasts convert malt sugars to alcohol at this rate. It's a part of nature — like water boiling at 100 degrees or two-stroke mowers only starting when they want to. Light-beer technology has allowed brewers to play with the traditional building blocks of beer and change the amount of alcohol — and flavour. Which is why, over the past two decades, light beers have been the way they have . . . a bit like Dolly the sheep . . .

The secret to light beer is to mimic the taste and feel of the alcohol in normal-strength beers. Brewers have to fake the 2.5% or so of alcohol that you're not getting. Remember, malt sugars make the alcohol, and the taste of beer comes from malt sugars. All sorts of tricks are employed to make you, the drinker, think that your light beer is still satisfying:

darker, more caramelised malt to impart colour and a richer flavour; yeasts that convert sugar to alcohol at a lower rate; extra hopping to lift aromas; and security-pass-access brewing-house frigging about that can only be compared to battery-farm egg production . . .

Techniques such as high-gravity brewing are being increasingly employed to make light beer more flavoursome. The process involves making high-strength beer at high temperatures then diluting it to make it lower in alcohol. If that sounds like the brewer is making you a non-sweet shandy, then you're listening very attentively. Speaking of shandies, that might be a better answer to your light-beer drinking dissatisfaction than a lot of the light beers doing the rounds. Another techie problem that confronts brewers when inventing lights concerns methional. This chemical is a by-product of yeast's ethanol manufacture. In normal-strength beer, the smelly methional is either eaten away or covered up by other chemical interactions, but in light beer, where the fermentation is stopped or short, the foul methional remains, giving light beers that dish-cloth smell so hated by beer drinkers.

Of course, light beer can also refer to beer low in calories. Good grief. How ridiculous is life becoming? There are about 150 calories in a normal-strength stubby; light is about 100, sometimes up to 120 calories. The difference amounts to a few peanuts or about three salt-and-vinegar chips . . . That's all we want to say about low-calorie beers.

But perhaps the most interesting thing to note about light or low-alcohol beers is the way their consumption is indeed growing. Drink-driving is forcing people into light-beer consumption, as is the general goody-goody approach to diet and health. You know: 'if I drink less alcohol I will be a better person' sort of guff. Normal-strength beer consumption is dropping; however, it's at about 70 litres per head per annum, whereas light — as we said — is growing. It's about 23 litres per head every year. Apparently, 25% of the beer we drink is light beer . . . Statistics are scary things: three in 10 people are also supposed to be teetotal . . .

All our cynicism aside, there are more good light beers now available than there were in the past. Vast slabs of this wide, amber-coloured land's culture have happily incorporated light and mid-strength beer into their lifestyle — with no slur on their sexuality. All the poofs have moved on to wine anyway . . .

Carlton Midstrength

Mid-strength Lager 375ml 3.5% alc vol

This is quite an achievement: a 3.5%-alcohol-by-volume beer that is not wanting in anything. Its medium body is a feature rather than a fault. The round, malty flavours trace through your mouth in a satisfying yet refreshing way. This beer is quite a pick-me-up. It might have something to do with the bitter hops' early attack — they seem to come in halfway through and carry the beer down your throat, before leaving a long, clean lick of muted astringency.

And another thing . . .

One 375ml stubby of Midstrength is one standard drink — or one middy of normal beer. Which means that if you intend to drive the chariot home, it's the old rule: no more than two standard drinks in the first hour for blokes (no more than one for blokettes), and no more than one every hour thereafter (up to a point, of course, so carefully does it . . .). Which on Midstrength means that after three hours of drinking you get, in volume terms at least, one free middy or pot. No wonder it's so successful.

LIGHT BEERS / 121

Carlton Sterling

Light 375ml 2.5% alc vol

Carlton and United have really got the light recipe right with this beer. It says on the label 'double hopped', and that's what it's all about. A pale golden yellow, it emits a fragrance of thirst-quenching, mild, unpolished steel. Maybe that's why they've given it the 'Sterling' moniker and stainless-steel-coloured label. Clever brewing trickery has given Sterling the semblance of a full-bodied, full-alcohol beer. There's barely a hint of light about it, and the bittering hops come tearing in at the end to finish things off before you've noticed anything missing.

And another thing . . .

Once the CUB brewers had perfected this fine light recipe, the job would have gone to the marketing people to develop the package. With a space-shuttle-shaped bottle, a name that recalls those Benson and Hedges cigarettes people smoked in the 1980s, a neck label we reckon is inspired by Crown Lager and with a red star like that on the Heineken label, here it is – brilliant . . .

Cascade Premium Light

Light 375ml 2.8% alc vol

With a real beer colour and appearance in the glass, this light is a pleasant surprise. It has the signature nose of Cascade Premium proper: slightly rich malt that reminds you a bit of Horlicks, balanced by some floral, spicy hops. Once swallowed, bittering hops encase the smooth flavour as it flows down the throat. The only sign that it's 2.8% alcohol is a hint of hollowness around the tonsils. It is a light you can drink and be satisfied with. Again and again. Very good light indeed.

And another thing . . .

Our world is obsessed with measuring. It wasn't long ago that the notion of alcohol by volume didn't even exist. Drinkers didn't know how many 'standard drinks' they'd had before they got on their horse backwards. Now in our calorie-obsessed, kilometres-per-litre, exercise-regimed, quality-timed lives, nothing can simply exist or be. Even one of man's greatest friends, beer, has an agenda.

Coopers Light

Light 375ml 2.9% alc vol

It's all nose, this beer, a bit like Sarah Jessica Parker, complete with an otherwise diminutive physique and lots of frizzy, floppy hair on top. It's a bit of a tease, too, because the taste doesn't live up to the smell. It leans to the front of the mouth as if it doesn't want to go down your throat, which is not a good thing because that's where all good beer goes — down. But it's refreshing and not a bad breakfast beer.

And another thing . . .

Devotees of Coopers ales shouldn't expect the same kind of rustic and characterful personality from this beer. For a start, this light is a lager, so it doesn't give you that mouthful of smooth, chewy ale texture. This one's all about refreshment, not flavour.

Foster's Light Ice

Light 375ml 2.5% alc vol

This is one of those light beers that makes you consider drinking heavy beers and getting a cab home (or out). It has all the hallmarks of a stereotypical 'lite'. While it looks like it's got the goods — amber colour, creamy head — the only thing your mouth registers is the temperature: cold, warm, whatever. (Actually, we would seriously advise against drinking this at anything less than near-freezing.) There is some beer-like flavour as it slips across your tongue but that's dilute, and its finish is empty and unsatisfying. There are better light beers.

And another thing . . .

A home-brewer couldn't make a beer like Light Ice in his or her shed. It has had all the fancy-pants brewing treatment, marketing, and advertising campaign guff thrown at it: ultra-high-gravity brewing and chill-filtering, a proprietary clear glass bottle . . . but to what avail?

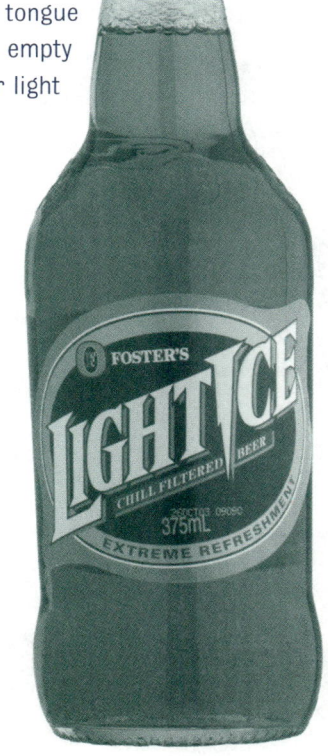

Hahn Premium Light

Light 375ml 2.7% alc vol

The colour of Hahn standard, this beer looks right but problems arise as soon as the aromas are assessed. In fact, we recommend that if you want to drink this beer you don't bother smelling it. All we can say is it smells beer-like, but with a hint of the chemistry lab kicking in. We say on page 129 that Tooheys Blue (at only 2.5%) reminds us of good pub tap beer; well, this reminds us of bad pub tap beer. It's a semblance of the real thing: lifeless and unfinished, like a circle that doesn't quite join up.

And another thing . . .

This beer claims its 'dryness' as one of its strengths . Genuinely dry-style beers — like Asahi on page 24 -- use dryness on top of flavour to make for a quenching drink. Because this light lacks the punch of flavour (which is the curse of light beer) its dryness comes across as nothing more than emptiness.

James Boag's Premium Light

Light 350ml 2.9% alc vol

Mr Boag's Premium Light has the pale golden colour of a German lager, but the first thing you notice is its aroma of creamed honey (Capilano, we think) atop a bed of spicy hop flowers. This honeyed, hazelnutted richness — courtesy of the maltings — continues inside your mouth. Just when the connoisseur begins to worry that the beer might cloy, the hop spice and bitterness grab the reins — and the insides of your cheeks — balancing everything out with an attractive astringency.

And another thing . . .

Package sizes. We've talked in this chapter already about our world's obsession with measuring the percentage of alcohol, but what about volume? 375ml, 330ml, 345ml, 350ml, 440ml in a can? Where light beers are concerned, volume is often manipulated to make the product fit in with 'standard drink' orthodoxy — such as 'Contains 0.8 standard drinks'. And then there's the question of excise on alcohol . . . Brewery accountants know all about $ margin at volume . . .

LIGHT BEERS / 127

Swan Mid Lager

Mid-strength Lager 375ml 3.5% alc vol

This mid-strength Western Australian is polite. He's an accountant in a large firm; he shaves every day and dabs his fresh, pink cheeks with a splash of Paco Rabanne, which his sister gave him for his birthday . . . a very long time ago. He (let's call him Lionel) crosses the t's and dots the i's, and is good for a five-minute chat, but 10 minutes is too much. He's not easy to dislike, but he's hard to like. When he (very occasionally) has a sickie, the people at work don't even know he's missing. Poor Lionel.

And another thing . . .

The way this bloke uses after-shave is a bit like the way the brewers of this beer have used late-gifted hops. The little bit of exotic perfume is derived from the brewers chucking in some aromatic hops right at the end of the brewing process. It gives the beer a bit of a lift, and masks a few less-than-savoury brewing odours.

Tooheys Blue Bitter

Light 375ml 2.5% alc vol

With a paradoxical dark copper colour (remember, it's a light beer) Tooheys Blue impresses you immediately with its front-bar, tap-beer aroma. It smells like the real thing — a pub. A good pub. It's fresh, clean, generously bittered and it offers your mouth some texture, something to chew on. The missing 2.5% of alcohol shows up in your mouth, but it's actually a feature. It makes for refreshment. You could down it all day and still be satisfied. Light beer has come a long way.

And another thing . . .

Indeed it has come a long way. Remember those thin, pissy, caramelised 'lites' of a few years ago? The improvements are thanks to advances in brewing technology and the ever-curious minds of otherwise beer-befuddled brewers. Such things as 100% malt decoctions, high residual carbohydrates, and adjunct replacement protocols . . .

LIGHT BEERS / 129

Tooheys Gold

Mid-strength Lager 375ml 3.2% alc vol

Mid-strength beer is not bad stuff at all. This Gold manages to lightly step on every beer-flavour receptor as it goes through your mouth; there's certainly nothing heavy-handed or powerful about it, but it does manage to fake the effect of full-strength beer quite well. With a bit of honey on the nose, a Weight Watchers kind of maltiness and body in your mouth, and — arguably, its most prominent feature — some unabashed bitterness up the back, it's quite a quencher.

And another thing . . .

Cans versus stubbies? Which is best for beer enjoyment? We've asked Australia's leading brewers and the consensus is that it doesn't matter. Cans don't break, they can be cooled more quickly, they cut out the harmful effect of UV light, and they're fun to crush. Glass, on the other hand, is a better insulator, is better to drink from, but can be used as a missile or primitive hunting tool . . .

130 / **LIGHT BEERS**

XXXX Gold Lager

Mid-strength Lager 375ml 3.5% alc vol

The only nice thing we have to say about this beer is its colour. It is gold. It is beer-like. But most of all, it is an industrial product. The aroma is a mixture of Sunlight soap and clumsily infused hops. It wouldn't matter how much you chilled this beer it still wouldn't satisfy. Maybe it should be tried frozen. Not a beer for men – a beer for brutes . . .

And another thing . . .

Queensland is one of those states that has gone apeshit over mid-strength beer. With less alcohol, Queenslanders can drink more of this amber fluid, and that's what hot weather is all about. Demographic studies indicate people move to Queensland for the climate and resultant thirst. It just seems that the beer quality is not that important.

LIGHT BEERS

Chapter Six
Weirdo Beers

There would be no normal if there were no abnormal. The avant garde wouldn't exist without the garde. The mainstream wouldn't be the mainstream without subsidiary rivulets branching off. It's the balance of things: in nature, in society, and in beer.

If you consider for a moment the beer world as a school playground, the beers in this chapter are the weird kids — the weird kids you find in every school. They're not like the rest. Some are naughty, some are misunderstood, some are foreigners who are hard to decipher, yet amongst them there might be a child genius. Whatever the case may be, it's both silly and dangerous to turn your back on these interesting kids. You can learn something from them, even if they're not your idea of modern youth.

We've got all these weird kids in this chapter. The bored soda-popped American boy known as Bud; the smelly, sweaty kid from Victoria, ironically named Carlton Dry; the obese Danish boy, Carl Sberg, known as the Elephant; a complex little blonde girl known as Leffe, and her serious older brother, Vieille. There's an awkwardly dressed and slightly stuttering Czech boy named Urquell; an orphaned South Australian the other kids just call 107; a Gold Coaster (whose dad owns an outboard motor dealership), Castlemaine Perkins; and the tall Japanese kid, Sapporo, who's into glam rock.

It's a weird and wonderful playground. Lagers, bocks, dry beers, white beers, aged beers, doppel-bocks, high-alcohol jobs, diet beers, and standard beers that went a bit awry.

The criteria we used for inclusion in this chapter were broad. Some beers were of high quality but so strange in either their style or taste that they had no other chapter to go into. Others were just ridiculous in either execution or effect. If you take your time to read your way through these reviews you'll soon work it out for yourself, though.

The important thing to remember is that whether these beers are good, bad or ugly, just as some subsidiary rivulets do flow on and join the mainstream, some of these beers do develop or become slowly more popular, thus helping the evolution of beer tastes and styles in Australia.

Aventinus

Wheat doppel-bock 500ml 8% alc vol

This beer takes the weirdo cake. Not only is it a wheat beer, it's also a doppel-bock. And it tastes like a medieval cure-all. Cloudy mahogany in colour, it has an aroma of caraway, rye bread, mixed peel, yeast and caramel. It's quite a concoction, even a bit scary — and that's just the smell. If you're brave enough to taste it, this beer is chewy and fruity in a stewy sort of way. The amazing thing about it — given everything that's going on — is its dry, evaporating finish. There's nothing cloying or sickly sweet about it. Another winter's night job.

And another thing . . .

G. Schneider and Sons, the brewery responsible for Aventinus, has been around for more than a century, and this beer is the original wheat doppel-bock. There's no doubt that this beer is more suited to Germany's climate than Australia's, but we do have the occasional cold front, the odd dark night, and ski resorts that sometimes have snow.

Budweiser

Lager 355ml 4.9% alc vol

We don't know why this is in the book; it's almost not beer. Having said that, it's the world's leading beer brand — yet another indication of how silly the planet is at present. It's floral but confectionery-floral; it's smooth enough, but watery. This beer has about as much integrity as a UDL vodka-orange or a cup of instant coffee. If you haven't been paying attention, we don't like this beer. It's made to be sessional but is simply tasteless. This is a weird beer in that it is so popular. We don't get it.

And another thing . . .

Budweiser proudly claims on its neck label that it is the 'King of Beers'. Just like a lot of kings, Bud has completely failed to realise that a revolution — in this case, the beer revolution — has come and gone. And just like the last prince of an exhausted family line, the three things that beer needs (good malt, water and hops) have been entirely bred out. The beer world is not a monarchy any more.

WEIRDO BEERS / 137

Carlsberg Elephant Beer

Lager 330ml 7.2% alc vol

The vast majority of beers tend to be about 5% alcohol by volume. They all seem to do the job, so to speak. This Elephant Beer from Carlsberg in Denmark weighs in at 7.2%. This doesn't change the aroma that much (although Elephant is more malty than Carlsberg standard), but what it does do is make the mouth feel a bit racier and the flavours bigger and more fruity. Perhaps the elephant on the label is a metaphor? They do like to drink . . .

And another thing . . .

Jacob Jacobsen, the founder of Carlsberg, was a bit of a weird bloke. After going to great lengths to establish his brewery in 1847 and building it up to be one of Europe's best, he created the Carlsberg Foundation in 1876. The foundation took over the brewery after his death and, ever since, all of Carlsberg's profits have gone to artistic charities. So if you're an artist — even a piss artist — and you drink Carlsberg, you're effectively self-funded.

Carlton Premium Dry

Lager 355ml 4.9% alc vol

How did this one get out of CUB's trial lab? It's one of the weirdest beers we tasted in this book's trials. With a sweet-and-sour and sulphury nose reminiscent of bad takeaway Chinese, cap guns and farts, and a taste and texture more like a beer-based eggnog, it had us shaking our heads in disbelief — and belief. I guess we've seen enough of the hideous creatures big breweries can occasionally produce, Doctor-Moreau-style. Unfortunately, such beers are not so much of a surprise . . .

And another thing . . .

Why did CUB put a beer on the market that smells like farts? Well, weird things can happen when brewers are given briefs based on perceived market forces and hypothetical niches. 'Macka, we need a dry beer to match that Tooheys shit. We need it by Friday or heads are gonna roll. Make it like theirs but with a twist — and better.' The door of the trial brewery closes and the marketing genius walks smugly back to his office. Macka the brewer fires up the brew kettle . . .

WEIRDO BEERS

Castlemaine Perkins Sovereign

Lager 375ml 3.8% alc vol

Talk about hard to drink — with any pleasure at least. This 'superior lager' is a bits-and-pieces beer, a two-headed beer monster. One head is screaming out sickly, almost unfermented malt-syrup flavours; the other is letting rip with caramelised bananas. We know it's from Queensland but this is ridiculous. Not even the hops charging in at the death help. They're swamped by creamy caramel. This beer lacks length and drinkability. Not recommended.

And another thing . . .

Premium, superior lagers are not just beers with shitloads of overstated ingredients — more malt, more hops, even more malt, some unfermented malt, and so on. Good beer is about subtlety and fine integration of flavours — that is, restraint. Steaks don't get better the more you cook them on the barbie; beer doesn't get better the more ingredients you chuck in it.

Chimay 2002

Bottle-conditioned Ale 330ml 9% alc vol

This dark ale is full of wild blackcurrant and cocoa powder aromas set off by a strange whiff of smoked oysters. Weird indeed. It's nevertheless enticing — or at least interesting — and slides into your mouth to offer more blackcurrant, Belgian chocolate and coffee flavours. It's as smooth as a monk's tonsure. Vintage-dated 2002, it comes in a 330ml bottle (like this one) and in a 750ml champagne-cork-stoppered bottle. Both can be cellared for a few years to further its integration and enhance its silky smoothness.

And another thing . . .

You might think that the 750ml champagne-cork-stoppered bottle would have more cachet than the plain old 330ml bottle, but there is a danger. We opened the cork-stoppered one only to discover that the smell and taste had been ruined by the same cork mould that ruins up to 10% of bottled wine. The moral here: stick to crown seals.

Chimay Triple

Bottle-conditioned Ale 330ml 8% alc vol

Cloudy, top-fermented strong ale from a Belgian monastery, Chimay Triple is also known as blanche or white. Amber-coloured, with a creamy, even head, its aromas are reminiscent of spice racks and zested lemons. It has a dry, smooth, nutmeggy taste and texture that show fantastic integration. The nutmeggy finish goes on and on. It's quite seductive — very seductive, actually — but watch out for that 8% alcohol.

And another thing . . .

We've said quite often in this book that some beers are better drunk out of wineglasses in order to appreciate their complex aromas. Taste is mostly about smell — remember how when you have a bad head cold you can't seem to taste anything? Well, this beer's back label finally contains some useful information. There's a simple drawing of a beer glass sitting next to a wineglass. A big cross has been put through the beer glass. A simple and effective message.

142 / WEIRDO BEERS

Gösser Dark Beer

Dark Ale 330ml 4.2% alc vol

If you love Vegemite, Bonox, Promite and molasses you'll adore Gösser. It's the colour of a brown beer and has the aroma of the equestrian club's stud feed — the one with molasses mixed through it. It's plenty rich, with a big, broad palate and sweet finish. A snow-covered landscape, a log fire and a big overcoat would be the perfect environment for a Gösser Dark. It's difficult to imagine drinking it in the midst of summer — unless you're summering in Antarctica.

And another thing . . .

Austrian beers, such as Gösser Dark, tend to be sweeter and maltier than their Bavarian or Prussian counterparts. In Germany, beer brewing is governed by purity laws. However, the use of unmalted cereals is allowed in Austrian brewing.

WEIRDO BEERS / 143

Hoegaarden White

Wheat Beer 330ml 5% alc vol

In many ways this is more than a beer. It's an elixir. It looks healthy – sort of cloudy and mysterious, as if it's going to do you some good. Made up of wheat, barley and a tiny amount of oats, it's a veritable multi-grain mix. On top of that there's the spice and kick of coriander and curaçao, an orange-flavoured liqueur. In a way, it's a cocktail as well. It's certainly refreshing, but offers plenty of body, bite and grainy wholesomeness. The explanation for the latter characteristic is that the barley and oats are not malted but go in raw, to make something akin to wheat porridge. Weird, fantastic beer.

And another thing . . .

Hoegaarden don't make any bog-standard beers, which is pretty typical of Belgium, where beer takes the place of wine. Hoegaarden also make Grande Cru and Forbidden Fruit, which has a very lewd picture of Adam and Eve on the label. You can try these beers – and another famous Belgian beer, Leffe's – at Belgian beer cafes, which are starting to spring up in Australia's capital cities.

James Squire Original Pilsener

Pilsener 345ml 5% alc vol

This contemporary Australian pilsener style is a bit of a caricature of the real Czech pilsener deal. James has got all the fundamentals: big malt; mega zingy hoppiness; a bit of yeast complexity; and a bitter backbone. But everything is a little too generous. The malt is a tad sweet and cloying, the hops are a bit metallic (even a little rusty), and the yeast has turned the flavour of dried banana chips. Nevertheless, it does have flavour, unlike a lot of Australian 'Pilseners'.

And another thing . . .

While we might seem to have been a little critical, what the Malt Shovel Brewery, the maker of James Squire beers, is doing for Australian beers is to be applauded. For too long, Australian drinkers have survived on a beer diet of misnamed, misflavoured mistakes. James Squire beers are introducing drinkers to the new concept – flavour.

WEIRDO BEERS / 145

Leffe Blonde

Ale 330ml 6.6% alc vol

Few beers have a pedigree like this one. Indeed, beers such as this belong to their own unique style — they're called abbey beers. This one was first brewed at an abbey in Belgium in 1240, which was just a few years after the Magna Carta was signed in England. You can smell the history in the beer: big whiffs of cool, old stone cellars, macerated northern hemisphere fruits and berries, and leather-bound bibles. The taste of Leffe Blonde is rich and powerful, yet oddly refreshing, with a nicely sour finish. Definitely not a beer for a session, but it would be just right with an egg-and-bacon pie.

And another thing . . .

Some beers are social, others are not. Befitting its abbey and monks-cell origins we think this beer is well suited to quiet contemplation — contemplation of the beer, of God and the mysteries of belly-button fluff. For instance, why is it blue-coloured even when you wear an orange T-shirt? But, then again, why wear an orange T-shirt?

Leffe Vieille Cuvée

Brown Ale 330ml 8.1% alc vol

Some dogs are bred to look more like cats, some country-and-western singers are more rock, and this Belgian brown ale is nothing like the brown ales of the UK. It has double the alcohol, and is different in flavour and completely different in texture. The only thing similar is that it's brown. It's designed for a completely different purpose to English brown ale — sustenance rather than refreshment. Weirder still, we reckon this beer would be really good with pies. It's bronze-coloured, smells of rubbed herbs, old furniture, smoke and spice, and it follows through with a round, creamy and demanding mouthful of malt laced with infused hops.

And another thing . . .

This beer looks like it comes in a ceramic bottle — it seems to have been painted with something the texture of Mylanta. The faux-ceramic stubby is not just a marketing trick; it harks back to the time when this beer was bottled in earthenware vessels. Hang on, that is marketing, isn't it?

WEIRDO BEERS / 147

Pilsner Urquell

Pilsener 330ml 4.4% alc vol

With its dark golden colour and fine, creamy head, Pilsner Urquell is the originator from which all other pilseners were begotten. Nowadays, the many descendants don't resemble old grand-daddy Urquell much. He was born in 1842 and still tastes a bit 19th century, but he's an exciting beer. One stubby has a lot of stuff in it: tired old rivers, well-worn brewing equipment, drops of engine oil, and the brewer's lunch room — day-old bratwurst sandwiches and old washed-rind cheese lie on the table. And there's a metallic, hoppy gong that keeps clanging in your mouth long after the beer's been swallowed.

And another thing . . .

If you're bored by contemporary pilseners — with all their buttoned-up clean flavours and polite manners — get some of this product into you. Actually, it's not a product, or even a beer; it's a historical record full of fascinating titbits, such as the fact that it's lagered in old wooden barrels, not anal stainless steel.

Sapporo Original Draft Beer

Pilsener 650ml 5% alc vol

This Japanese beer is a clear, golden-coloured pilsener. Its taste and easy drinkability would make it a great sessional beer, but at about eight dollars a can the session would be over pretty quick. Sapporo smells of a freshly opened packet of rice cakes, which suggests that rice is used with barley in its production. The beer has a fine balance, an almost ethereal weight, and its flavours are so clean, light and polite that it's almost not there — a bit like really expensive sushi.

And another thing . . .

Lars is a 42-year-old retired architect. He drives a mint-condition 1963 Saab. He was married for a while to a Japanese supermodel called Camy, but that's all over now. He spends a lot of time at the gym, the tanning salon, and in upmarket bars. He drinks Sapporo as a sessional beer because he loves the taste, the design of the can and the fact that, at the end of the night, he can crush the cans between his bum cheeks. His mates, Renee and Stevie, find this hysterically funny.

WEIRDO BEERS / 149

Schneider Weisse The Original

Wheat Beer 500ml 5.4% alc vol

Many wheat-beer junkies consider this Schneider to be a classic of the style. It's the colour of a river after rain, or some pretty muddy dam water, and if you were served it in a pub, you'd send it back. But there's nothing wrong with it. The overtly yeasty, wheaty smell — raised a notch by that trace of lemon rind so typical of wheat beers — promises strength, health and a good time. And it's a racier time than you might expect. The wheat-grain flavour is enhanced by a lemony tang that reminds us of dark rye bread or sourdough. It's piquant and would probably go very well with rollmops.

And another thing . . .

Some people get off on wheat beer's perceived health-giving properties — all that unfiltered, bottle-conditioned cloudiness and left-over dead yeast. But all beer is good for you, isn't it?

Schöfferhofer Premium Weissbier

Wheat Beer 500ml 5% alc vol

The fact that this beer's made from a blend of malted barley and malted wheat is the only thing weird about it. It's as straight as a convertible BMW and similarly well-made. It's sturdy yet luxurious and handles very well around the oesophageal bends. The head is thick and creamy with a fine bubble typical of wheat beer, and there's a richness and depth which comes from the malted barley and yeast, balanced by a refreshing lemony zing from the wheat. It's a bit of a sweet-and-sour experience.

And another thing . . .

Wheat beer might seem weird in Australia but in places such as Bavaria, from which this beer comes, it's very much the norm, particularly in the German summer when the locals drink litres of it, their beer glasses garnished with slices of lemon. A slice of lemon is a good idea; it highlights wheat beer's lemony notes — and prevents scurvy.

WEIRDO BEERS / 151

Southwark Pale

Pale Ale 375ml 4.6% alc vol

We think this beer represents another typical brewing conundrum, as it was no doubt made to counter the popularity of fellow South Australian, Cooper's Pale Ale. But Southwark Pale has managed to carve out an entirely different niche. At the soy-sauce and Bonox end of ale-aroma orthodoxy, this cloudy, yellow-gold beer is rich, with a fairly lactic taste. It has that salted-butter aftertaste typical of much ale. It's chewy with quite a harsh bubble, and its saltiness makes it perfect with fish and chips, or with dim sims.

And another thing . . .

Three of Australia's most popular so-called pale ales — Southwark, Coopers, and Cascade — have green labels. Why? Green means go, green means peace, green means grass, green means envy, green means St Patrick . . . Green means Kermit the 'It's not easy being green' Frog. But probably green means naturally brewed and free of preservatives — or that's what it suggests.

Southwark White Beer

Wheat Beer 345ml 5% alc vol

With a fluffy head and cloudy, muted gold colour, this wheat beer is a good drink and a pleasant surprise. The smell and flavour are driven by iron-ore-like hoppy bitterness; there's even a bit of charcoal. And the fruit flavours are at the citrus end of the spectrum. Despite the plentiful hoppiness, it also has a creamy, silky body and texture. Its only fault is that it has a milky or lactic finish, but so do café lattes, and look how popular they are . . .

And another thing . . .

Southwark comes from South Australia. Over there, it's pronounced 'suthh-ick', so don't walk into an Adelaide pub and ask for a 'Southwark'. If you do, a member of the Gypsy Jokers will whack you over the head with a pool cue. South Australians are strange: they call telephone poles 'Stobies', devon sausages 'fritz', light showers 'floods', and small undulations on flat land 'hills'.

Tooheys Maxim

Low-calorie Lager 375ml 4.6% alc vol

Launched just before Christmas 2000, quite a lot of work has gone into the production of this beer. Not only does it contain 20% fewer calories than standard beers, it's been given a late gift of hops, which accounts for those lovely, exotic, drying minerally galvanised aromas. The smell is really very attractive and fruity. The palate disappoints a little though. This beer's simple, malty flavour sits at the front of your mouth, as if it doesn't want to go down.

And another thing . . .

Ben asked why this label had to look Russian. Greg replied that Tooheys' marketing gurus had done heaps of research and worked out that this label would appeal to stick-insect, diet-pill-swallowing chicks. But Ben insisted, 'No, it looks Russian – and the Russians love shitloads of calories.' To which Greg responded, 'No, Ben, it's about marketing; you don't understand . . .'

Tooheys Pils

Lager 345ml 5.2% alc vol

This smartly packaged product could have been a cracker — a real pilsener — if only they'd let the brakes off. Instead, as the name suggests, we've got half a beer. Having gone to all the trouble to tell us on the label that it's brewed with traditional Czech Saaz hops (the very hops that make Pilsener Pilsener), it's as if they've forgotten to put them in — or, at least, enough of them. It's more faartz than Saaz. It smells of freshly baked banana cake, the texture is milky, and its soft bite is gummy rather than incisive.

And another thing . . .

In our dealings with big breweries we've noticed that the marketing departments are sometimes unaware that their company has a brewing division. The left hand doesn't know what the right hand is doing. It's as if the marketing kids stumbled on this banana-cake-like brew and decided to put it in this bottle they'd designed over a particularly creative lunch.

WEIRDO BEERS / 155

West End 107 Pilsener

Pilsener 375ml 5% alc vol

We've put this pilsenser-style beer in the weirdo section for a few reasons. It's not really that weird, it just has a few odd things going on. For a start, it's quite a good, if simple, premium lager and it's from West End. They make a strong point on the label about their use of Saaz hops, the Czech Republic's famous, fragrant, nutty hop. The aroma is rich with honey, which carries through into your mouth, yet there's enough raciness from the hops to keep the beer relatively clean and easily drinkable. And 107? Weirder still.

And another thing . . .

We came up with lots of different theories about why this beer is called 107. Did they put 107 Saaz hop pellets in the kettle? Was this the 107th attempt to perfect this product? Or is it some weird South Australian sexual position? Perhaps a little beer-braindead, Greg gazed at the label and noticed the address of West End Brewery: 107 Port Road, Adelaide. How inspired . . .

Glossary

The words contained herein represent various parts of the Australian beer drinker's lexicon: technical terms, colloquialisms, pub lingo, jargon, expletives . . . (after all, a catalogue of beer terms should always include those words and phrases that perhaps should have been left at the bar). For definitions of beer styles, as used in this guide, see pages 5–7.

Aardvark: an animal whose name begins with two a's — often found at the beginning of any glossary. Also the name given to a South African yard-and-a-half glass taken through the nose.

Adjunct: any ingredient added to beer that's not malt, yeast or water; also a great descriptive term for any odd flavour in beer, life, food, whatever.

Alcohol: a form of medicine often misunderstood by family members.

All-nighter: an extreme sport fuelled by beer. Most capably performed by young men and women before any of the following realisations: mortality, consequences, STDs, and the difference between good beer and bad . . .

Amber: the colour of ale, also the middle colour of a traffic light. Both ask the same question: stop or go?

Arsehole: any member of the allied hospitality beverage-service-industry profession who refuses to serve you one more beer at 3am.

Bar: when you walk into a pub or hotel you will often notice a bench behind which barmen, barmaids and bar taps lurk. When you get to the bar, stop walking. Stay there for as long as it takes.

Beer: go to the front of the book and start again.

Beer goggles: according to moralists, these are imaginary spectacles through which people see the opposite sex in a more beautiful form – usually when they are blind.

Bender: down-time; relaxation.

Blind: inebriated.

Brewer's droop: see Foster's flop.

Brewery: no, not sure . . .

Bullshit: the talk overheard at any bar.

Cold Chisel: God's own beer band . . .

Conditioning: the process by which young beer drinkers convince themselves that shit sessional beers are OK; the process by which brewers settle and carbonate beer.

Decoction: a stew of boiling malt and hops; a vasectomy.

Dickhead: a mutual friend not present at the pub during discussion.

Doppel-bock: a stronger, more alcoholic version of bock; a bottom-fermented job; dark brown; the names of these beers usually end in 'ator'.

Empty: a sad thing — bar, beer glass, wallet, fridge . . .

Fat: beer is not fattening, bar snacks are.

Foster's flop: see Brewer's droop.

Gas: nitrogen used to put the bubbles in draught beer — also the bubbles that come out of the beer drinker.

Head: the frothy bit above the liquid action.

Hell: German word for 'pale'.

Kettle: huge copper vessel in which the wort is boiled.

Label: a source of misinformation attached to a stubby.

Ladies' lounge: mostly extinct.

Lambic: a wheat beer fermented by wild yeasts; more like wine than beer; see poof.

Late gift: technical term for when the brewer forgets his wife's birthday — also the late addition of hops.

Lauter tun: vessel used for lautering, or the filtering of wort; also a century scored by Germany's most famous cricketer Hans Lauter.

Light-struck: beer ruined by excessive exposure to UV light; cans and brown bottles best screen this.

Malt: germinated barley.

Mate: drinking companion whose name you're unfamiliar with, even though you've met him 93 times; also a form of verbal punctuation: 'Yeah, mate, I know mate. Mate, I agree, mate, yes, no worries mate . . .'

Münchner: Munich-style beer; a dark brown lager.

Nathan: beer fermenter that circulates carbon dioxide. Popular in Australian brewing and named after the bloke who invented it — he's German and no one can remember his last name.

Old: a dark ale.

Oktoberfest: beer-drinking festival in Germany where you will run into a lot of Australian footballers — all bliiiind.

Pale ale: top-fermented beer; pale in colour, as opposed to the darker brown of normal ales.

Pilsener: a type of lager with a stronger hop accent.

Pitching: brewers don't just chuck yeast into their Nathans, they pitch it.

Poof: wine drinker.

Pub: if you don't know, this book won't help.

Puke: to be ill from bar food.

Rauchbier: not a beer for seduction, but a beer using smoked malts; made in Franconia, Germany.

Recycling: un-Australian.

Shelf-life: for beer, about nine months — fresh is best.

Shout: any one person's turn to buy the round of beers two or more people are enjoying two or more pub.

rtable pack of beer which helps you leave d yet still embrace home life.

GLOSSARY / 163

Slab: the same drug as above but four times the power.

Stout: a top-fermented, black-brown ale made from highly roasted malts.

Stubby: something to start and end the day with.

Tab: the best and most generous-spirited way to manage one's cash outgoings when in a pub.

Trappist: Belgian monk whose religious calling involves beer drinking. Are all Australian men Trappists?

Trub: unwanted solids whirlpooled out of the wort during the boiling process.

Widget: a plastic container full of nitrogen found inside clever cans of tossy imported beer.

Wort: the term used to describe the malted barley and water mixture in the brewing process; nothing to do with toads.

Yeast: crucial organism without which there would be no fermentation, no beer and no Vegemite either.

INDEX

Ambar Cerveza Especial	62	Chimay 2002	141
Asahi Super 'Dry'	24	Coopers Best Extra Stout	105
Aventinus	136	Coopers Light	124
Beamish Genuine Irish Stout	103	Coopers Original Pale Ale	32
Beck's Beer	25	Coopers Sparkling Ale	66
Bitburger Premium Beer	63	Coopers Special Old Stout	106
Boag's Strongarm Bitter	26	Corona Extra	33
Boddingtons Pub Ale	27	Crown Lager	67
Budweiser	137	DAB Original	68
Caffrey's Premium Beer	28	Emu Bitter	34
Carlsberg Beer	64	Foster's Lager	35
Carlsberg Elephant Beer	138	Foster's Light Ice	125
Carlton Cold	29	Gösser Dark Beer	143
Carlton Draught	30	Grolsch Premium Lager	69
Carlton Midstrength	121	Guinness Draught	107
Carlton Premium Dry	139	Hahn Ice	36
Carlton Sterling	122	Hahn Premium	70
Cascade Pale Ale	31	Hahn Premium Light	126
Cascade Premium Lager	65	Heineken Lager	71
Cascade Premium Light	123	Hoegaarden White	144
Castlemaine Carbine Stout	104	Holsten Premium Beer	37
Castlemaine Perkins Sovereign	140	J. Boag's Original Bitter	38
Chimay Triple	142	James Boag's Premium	72

James Boag's Premium Light	127	Sapporo Original Draft Beer	149
James Squire India Pale Ale	109	Schneider Weisse The Original	150
James Squire Original Amber Ale	108	Schöfferhofer Premium Weissbier	151
James Squire Original Pilsener	145	Sheaf Stout	113
James Squire Porter	110	Singha Thai Beer	47
Kilkenny Draught	39	Southwark Bitter	48
Kingfisher Premium Lager	73	Southwark Old Stout	114
Kirin Beer	74	Southwark Pale	152
Labatt Blue	75	Southwark Premium Lager	80
Leffe Blonde	146	Southwark White Beer	153
Leffe Radieuse	111	Steinlager	81
Leffe Vieille Cuvée	147	Stella Artois	49
Little Creatures Pale Ale	90	Swan Draught	50
Little Creatures Rogers' Beer	91	Swan Mid Lager	128
Löwenbräu Original	76	Tetley's English Ale	51
Matilda Bay Premium	92	Tiger Beer	82
Melbourne Bitter	40	Tooheys Blue Bitter	129
Miller Genuine Draught	41	Tooheys Extra Dry	52
Mountain Goat Hightail Ale	93	Tooheys Gold	130
Mountain Goat India Pale Ale	94	Tooheys Maxim	154
Mountain Goat Pale Ale	95	Tooheys New	53
Nastro Azzurro	77	Tooheys Old	115
Newcastle Brown Ale	42	Tooheys Pils	155
Oakbank Beer	96	Tooheys Red Bitter	54
Old Speckled Hen	43	Tsingtao Beer	83
Paulaner Original Münchner	78	Tuborg Gold Label	84
Paulaner Salvator	112	Victoria Bitter	55
Pilsner Urquell	148	Warsteiner	85
Redback Original	97	West End Draught	56
Reschs Original Pilsener	44	West End 107 Pilsener	156
Reschs Real	45	XXXX Bitter	57
Samuel Adams Boston Lager	79	XXXX Gold Lager	131
San Miguel Super Dry	46		

About the authors

Ben Canaider is a Melbourne-based lifestyle journalist and occasional TV presenter, although he is yet to actually purchase a television . . . he's waiting for new technology. He drives a 1984 Ford Courier called Wayne and writes about alcoholic beverages for newspapers and magazines such as *The Age*, ABC's *delicious*, and *Offshore Yachting*. With Greg he co-authors *Drink Drank Drunk*, an annual guide to the best 150 wines in Australia. His favourite beer is Coopers Original Pale Ale.

Greg Duncan Powell lives in a remote part of south-coast New South Wales. He drives a Mazda Bravo called Rosie and arguably owns the largest collection of De Armond guitars in the southern hemisphere. He is the drinks editor for *Vogue Entertaining + Travel*, *Australian Table*, and several leading beer journals.

Both are keen cyclists (of the mountain-bike variety), but hate high-fiving. Both love T-bone steaks, but not supermarket meat sections. Ben likes the city and bars; Greg likes the country and his own fridge . . . their credit-card statements reflect this difference.